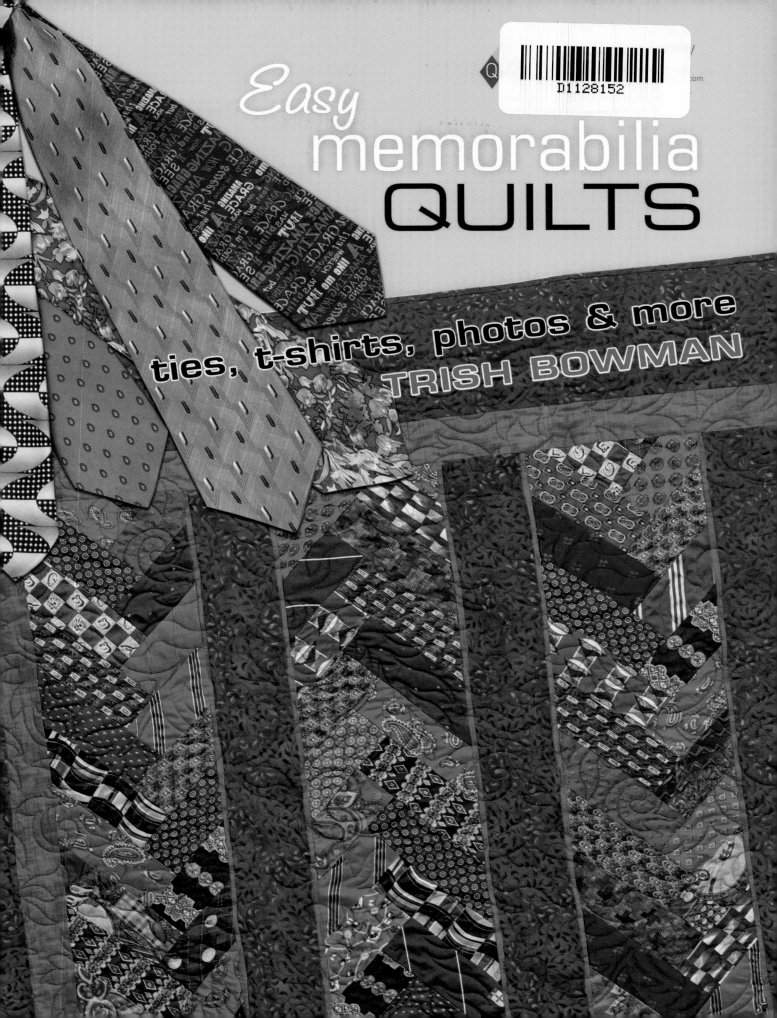

Easy
memorabilia
QUILTS

ties, t-shirts, photos & more
TRISH BOWMAN

Located in Paducah, Kentucky, the American Quilter's Society (AQS) is dedicated to promoting the accomplishments of today's quilters. Through its publications and events, AQS strives to honor today's quilt-makers and their work and to inspire future creativity and innovation in quiltmaking.

EXECUTIVE BOOK EDITOR: ANDI MILAM REYNOLDS
SENIOR BOOK EDITOR: LINDA BAXTER LASCO
GRAPHIC DESIGN: ELAINE WILSON
COVER DESIGN: MICHAEL BUCKINGHAM
HOW-TO PHOTOGRAPHY: TRISH BOWMAN
QUILT PHOTOGRAPHY: CHARLES R. LYNCH

Additional copies of this book may be ordered from the American Quil-ter's Society, PO Box 3290, Paducah, KY 42002-3290, or online at www.AmericanQuilter.com.

Text © 2013, Author, Trish Bowman
Artwork © 2013, American Quilter's Society

American Quilter's Society
P.O. Box 3290 • Paducah, KY 42002-3290
Fax 270-898-1173 • e-mail: orders@AQSquilt.com

Library of Congress Control Number: 2013930718

dedication

To my husband, Doug, who is my high school sweetheart, best friend, and soul mate. You have supported me in so many ways I can't even begin to express. I love you from the bottom of my heart and am forever grateful God brought you into my life.

To my children, Christopher, Jennifer, and Michael. You are all such wonderful people and I am so proud to call you mine. Thank you for all your love and support. It means so very much.

acknowledgments

I would like to thank the many people who have helped me get to the point in my life where I could write this book:

First of all, my sister Pam. Without her love and support throughout my life I would not be the person I am. She doesn't always agree with me but is there for me nonetheless. She is not just my sister, but also my best friend and I will be forever grateful for her being in my life.

The rest of the Bowman and Nudd family. I love you all and am so thankful to have you all in my life.

My quilting sisters, Vinell, Chris, Jane, Roberta, and Maryann (who was taken from us much too early). You have helped to make me the quilter I am today through love, laughter, and wonderful suggestions. I cherish our times together and wish for many more years of the same.

Nancy Prince, who started out as someone I knew and greatly admired in our quilt guild. By her example she helped me to push myself to think outside the box. She is a wonderful mentor and now friend whom I cherish. Her support and guidance helped me get this book from concept to publication. Without her this book would have never been finished. Thank you.

My Virginia family, the Wells, Hoggards, and Davises. You have been there for us sharing good times and bad, through raising our children and all our assorted jobs and businesses. Your unconditional love and support through the years have meant a great deal. Thank you, I love you all.

AQS executive book editor, Andi Reynolds, thank you for accepting my book and making my dream come true. Your support and guidance was wonderful and made the nerve-wracking process of writing a book and meeting deadlines much easier.

Last but not least, my editor, Linda Lasco. You took my designs and thoughts and pulled them all together into a beautiful package. Thank you.

contents

Note: If permission was not received to use an image or logo from a memorabilia piece, the photo of that block is intentionally blurred. Quilts made for your personal use do not require such permissions.

SAILING THE OCEAN BLUE project starts on page 53.

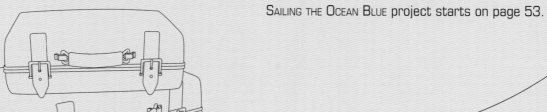

Easy Memorabilia QUILTS: *ties, t-shirts, photos & more* – Trish Bowman

making memories last

EASY MEMORABILIA QUILTS: TIES, T-SHIRTS, PHOTOS & MORE is all about how to make quilts that evoke memories. We have so many things around our homes that bring back memories of wonderful times in our lives—clothes, pictures, patches, etc. Memory quilts are a way of taking those items out of their hiding places so you can see them every day. I am very sentimental and love to snuggle under such a quilt and let the memories flow. I enjoy making them for myself and for other people as well.

Many people have said to me that there is no way they could ever make a memory quilt. That is simply not true. If you can sew clothes or quilts, then you can make a memory quilt. Through my experiences over the years of making all kinds of memory quilts, I have discovered ways to make the process easier. Look for "Trish's Tips" that pass on tricks of the trade and some of the lessons I've learned.

There are as many ways to make a quilt from your memories as there are memories themselves. I will show you how you can take just about any item and modify it to go into a quilt. I include quilt designs that integrate panels, appliqué, and embroidery to demonstrate the diversity of techniques that can be used. The sashing designs in I PLAY WITH TRAINS (page 32) and REACH FOR THE STARS (page 42) can be used to make a variety of memory quilts. Most of the designs are flexible and come in an array of sizes—from a smaller wallhanging perfect for photos or for displaying your memories and awards, to a large size suitable for that big guy or a couple to snuggle under on a cold winter's night. Part of the fun is choosing which variations to try.

I provide examples of how to take the theme of the design from the front and continue it onto the back of the quilt. This is taken even further with examples of personalized labels that carry the theme of the quilt with a special message or just the documentation of the quilter. When making these memory quilts I encourage you to think creatively and add your own embellishments, whether it is appliqué, embroidery, beads, buttons—whatever you enjoy working with.

Designing and making quilts for other people is exciting because everyone has a different personality that comes through in the fabrics they pick for the sashing, borders, and backing, as much as in the items they pick to put in the quilt itself.

Once you find out how much fun and how easy it really is to turn memories into quilts, I am sure you will be making many wonderful memory quilts for your family and friends.

Happy Memories!

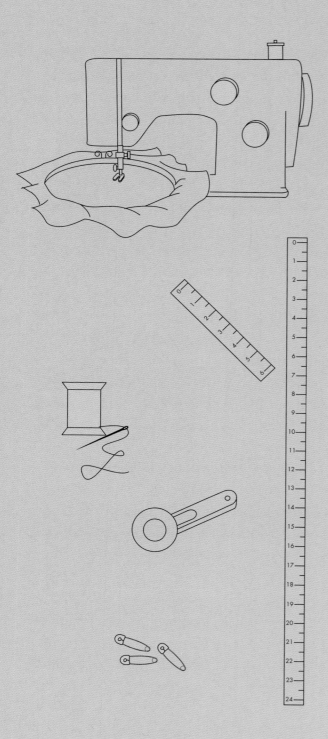

Having the right tools makes any project easier and more fun. A lot of the items listed here can be found at your local sewing stores. I sell many of them on my website, www.TrishBowman.com. If you have any questions, or difficulty finding something, feel free to contact me. I will be happy to help you.

Sewing machine – Any sewing machine that can sew a ¼" seam will work fine. It is helpful if you have a ¼" **presser foot**. An **open-toe presser foot** is not a requirement but it does make appliqué much easier as you can see exactly what you are stitching.

Embroidery machine – Embroideries are optional and you can always use washable pens instead. If you don't have embroidery capability on your machine, think about offering to do a binding for a friend while they do your embroideries on their machine.

All Squared Up Tee's Templates – For cutting T-shirts to their proper sizes, I offer a set of templates that I designed in 12½", 13½", 14½", 15½", and 16½" sizes. I also have 4½" and 5½" sizes for cutting small front designs from shirts and hats. T-shirts can also be trimmed to size using standard square rotary cutting rulers. (See Resources, page 94.)

Rulers – You will need a 24" ruler to cut strips and a 6" ruler for smaller cuts and marking lines.

Thread – I use either matching thread or gray, which blends well with most colors. For embroidery and appliqué, I use 40-weight thread. For appliqué I find the color that matches the closest to the fabric of the appliqué itself. You want it to disappear and not take away from what you are appliquéing.

Tricot stabilizer – A good tricot stabilizer is a must. When properly applied according to the manufacturer's directions, it will stabilize knits and other stretchy fabrics, making them much easier to work with.

Shades SoftFuse™ – I prefer SoftFuse for attaching small pieces to T-shirts and for appliqué. It does not add stiffness or weight to fabrics you are using.

Rotary cutter and mat

Appliqué pressing sheet – This is a must for when you are applying tricot and SoftFuse to protect the ironing board from the adhesives.

Chalk markers/Clover® Chaco Liners – These draw a fine line and get right up next to the ruler for accuracy. They come in four different colors. I use a yellow for dark fabrics and blue for light ones.

Clearly Perfect Angles – This is a wonderful tool that attaches by clinging to your sewing machine base. It makes sewing angles a breeze without having to take the time to draw a lot of chalk marks on your fabrics. (See Resources, page 94.)

Iron and ironing board – Any ironing board and iron will do as long as the iron will do both dry heat and steam.

Lettered safety pins – These are for marking rows of blocks and keeping them together once stacked. They are easy on and off and help make sure that rows and blocks don't end up in the wrong place. I use them constantly in my quilting.

Pressing cloths – I use one-ply diapers to press T-shirts to protect the designs on them. I also use them wet for applying tricot. They are the perfect weight for providing the right amount of dampness.

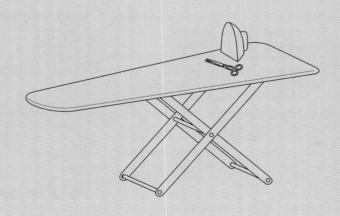

making a fabric shopping guide

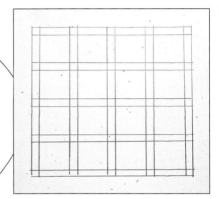

Fig. 1. Sample paper layout of a quilt

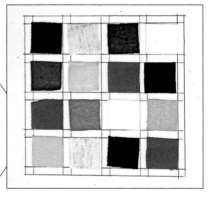

Fig. 2. Arrange the fabric squares on the plastic page protector.

This is a great idea I got from my friend Connie Small. It works really well and is such a time saver. This not only assists you in buying the right fabrics for your quilt, but also helps you to easily balance color and determine the best layout for the blocks. In addition, it helps decrease the moving of the full-size blocks later when finalizing the layout of your quilt.

a) Cut 1"–2" squares of fabric from portions of shirts or other items not destined for the quilt blocks themselves.

b) On a piece of paper draw the layout for your quilt. Include the correct number of blocks and leave space between and around the blocks for the sashing (Fig. 1).

c) Slide this layout into a plastic page protector.

d) Audition the fabric squares on the layout to find the most pleasing arrangement. Once you have decided your final arrangement, attach the fabric squares to the protector on top of the layout with double-stick tape (Fig. 2).

e) Take the guide with you to go fabric shopping. While shopping, pull the paper out of the plastic and lay the protector sheet on fabrics you are considering. You will be able to audition the various fabrics with all the different shirt colors without having to carry them all with you to the store (Fig. 3).

Fig. 3. Use the Fabric Shopping Guide to help find fabrics that coordinate with the blocks.

Easy Memorabilia QUILTS: *ties, t-shirts, photos & more* – Trish Bowman

making memories into blocks

In this section you will learn how to select and prepare just about any piece of memorabilia you may want to put in your quilt. For the best results, browse through the text completely before starting to design your quilt for an overview of the process.

Identify shirts and other memorabilia to be used in the quilt

Gather up the items that hold wonderful memories for you. Go through all your closets and drawers as well as those boxes stored under the beds, in the garage, attic, or basement. This is so much fun because you will find things you have forgotten about that are perfect for your quilts. I totally revamped a quilt design based on a shirt I found in the back of a closet. I would have kicked myself if I had found it after the quilt was done.

Pull out old shirts, sweatshirts, shorts, patches, hats—anything that brings back long ago or current memories. Don't think of a specific quilt yet, just collect everything you think you might want in a quilt—for yourself, your children, or whomever—and set it aside. Enjoy the process and don't rush. Allow yourself time to reminisce along the way! It is so exciting to go through your things and have long-lost memories rekindled.

Trish's Tip: If you don't have a specific item that you would like to include in a quilt, go online and order it. It may be a shirt from a place you visited but didn't think to get at the time or you did get one but it was lost. The idea is to bring back the memory, not just to use old stuff.

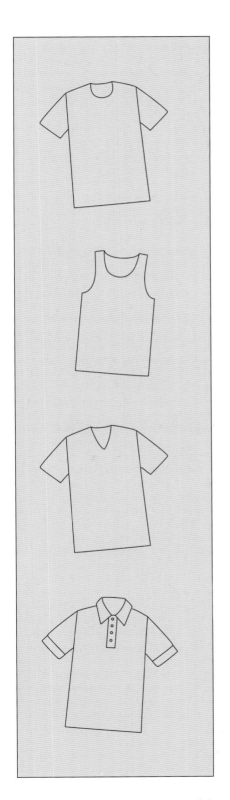

Clean away any stains or odors from storage

Wash everything as you normally would. Do not worry if all the stains don't come out; these add character and memories of their own to the quilt. My kid's soccer jerseys will forever hold Virginia clay from all their games and tournaments. I see these stains today in their memory quilts and, for us, they bring back some wonderful memories.

Organize the items by person and quilt themes

Separate everything you have collected into piles according to how you are thinking of putting them into a quilt—by person or by theme such as concerts, trips, sports, scouts, etc. I have done quilts for one specific trip a client went on with her daughter and I have done quilts that cover multiple trips. There is no right or wrong; it is whatever you want it to be.

Once all your items are sorted, package them accordingly so as not to mix them up between projects. Labeled, under-bed storage bins are a great way to keep things organized. Separating the items within the bin according to theme will save you from re-sorting when you are ready for your next quilt.

Decide what will go into the quilt

In evaluating your T-shirts, remember to look on the front, back, and sleeves for designs to use. Look at small logos or emblems that contain information not in the main design that can be sewn onto the main design to make the memory complete. Make a note as to which areas will be used and pin it to the shirt.

Determine your quilt size

Once you know how many items you have, the quilt size, as far as number of blocks, can be determined. The patterns for both I PLAY WITH TRAINS (pages 32–41) and REACH FOR THE STARS (pages 42–52) have charts for quilts with different numbers of different block sizes.

Initially, figure one item per block. If you have more items than what will fit into the size you have in mind, you can merge several items into a single block so that everything can be included. Label and pin items to be put together so you will know what to keep and what not to keep when you are cutting things apart later. Good organization early on is paramount to lessen the frustration when construction begins.

Merging two or more pieces of memorabilia requires a little extra thought.

Small items can be sewn together to make one block.

Small designs, such as the year of an event, can be cut out and sewn onto a larger design from the front or back of a shirt.

Sort according to the size of the design

Sort shirts according to the size of the designs on them. Determine what size to cut your blocks by finding the largest design. The various sizes of my All Squared Up Tee's Templates (see Resources, page 94) are perfect to evaluate each shirt design and decide on a size for the final blocks, or you can use square rotary cutting rulers. All the blocks in the quilt will ultimately be the same size, determined by the largest design to be used.

You can deal with the case where there are only a few shirts with bigger designs and you don't want to use a larger size for all the blocks in one of two ways:

• Cut the larger shirts down a little so all the shirt blocks are the same size.

• If cutting the shirts smaller will destroy the design, make the blocks in one row longer to accommodate these larger designs. Simply cut the blocks for that row longer and match the sashing strips along the sides to that measurement.

IMPORTANT – When changing the size of a block, the only requirement for these quilt designs to work is that all the blocks in the quilt must be the same width and all the blocks in any single row must be the same length (Fig. 1).

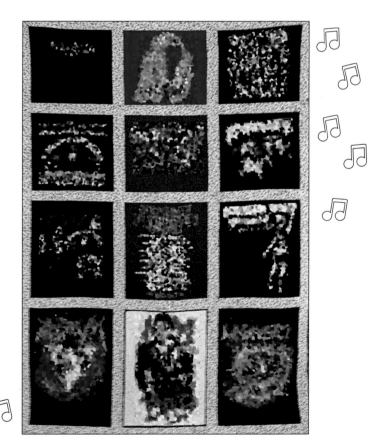

Fig. 1. Rows of different lengths accommodate larger-design shirts.

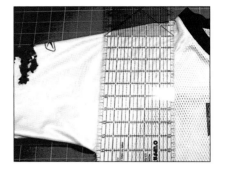

Fig. 2. Cut along the sleeve seams.

Fig. 3. If there is no sleeve seam, cut straight up from the side of the shirt.

Cut the memorabilia for the quilt

This can be an emotional time, cutting apart your memory items, but remember you are taking them out of the dark and making them into something that can be enjoyed every day. Just take a deep breath and go for it!

T-Shirts

a) Cut the sleeves off at the seams. If there are no seams in the arms just cut straight up from the side seam (Figs. 2–4).

b) Cut along the shoulder seams through the collar.

c) Open up the T-shirt so that the armholes are in the center. Cut the side seams. Set aside the parts of the shirt you will be using (Figs. 5–6).

Keep the large unused pieces of shirts such as plain fronts or backs. Blocks can be made from these to display smaller items in the quilt such as tank tops, patches, etc.

Fig. 4. Shirt with the sleeves cut off

Fig. 5. Cut straight up the side seams.

Fig. 6. The shirt front is ready to be made into a block.

Trish's Tip: If you are adding a sleeve or chest logo to the portion of the shirt that you are making into a block, pin these items onto the shirt now so they don't get lost or forgotten.

Cut a 1"–2" square of fabric from the smaller leftover scraps of each of the shirts you will be using. Set them aside for use when you're selecting background and sashing fabrics (see Making a Fabric Shopping Guide, page 10).

Square-up the shirts

Now you need to square up the shirts, cutting the blocks 1" larger overall than what the *unfinished* dimension will be. This allows for the block to be squared-up again after applying the tricot stabilizer, doing any appliqué, or combining any shirts, which can sometimes warp the blocks out of shape.

Dimensions for the initial squaring-up are as follows:

Initial Squaring-Up	Unfinished Block Size	Finished Block Size
16½" x 16½"	15½" x 15½"	15" x 15"
15½" x 15½"	14½" x 14½"	14" x 14"
14½" x 14½"	13½" x 13½"	13" x 13"
13½" x 13½"	12½" x 12½"	12" x 12"

a) Place a square ruler marked with the initial squaring-up dimensions or a template of the correct size on the shirt and line up the center with the center of the design (Fig. 7).

b) Straighten the design as much as possible by using the horizontal and vertical lines on the ruler or template as a reference. Some shirts become really warped due to washing and can't be straightened. This will just add character to the quilt (Fig. 8).

c) Make sure the design you want to see on the quilt is ¼" inside the inner solid square on the template all the way around. This assures what is seen through the template is the design that will be seen when it is sewn into the quilt (Fig. 9).

d) Cut around the template (Fig. 10).

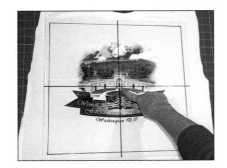

Fig. 7. Use a template or square ruler to find the center of the design.

Fig. 8. Straighten the design in the block.

Fig. 9. Make sure the design is inside the lines of the template.

Fig. 10. Cut the shirt to the initial squaring-up size.

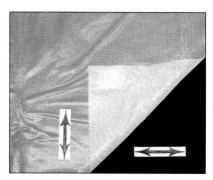

Fig. 11. Lay the tricot cross-grain to fabric.

Front view of the shirt

Back view of the shirt
Fig. 12. Shirt with two smaller designs

Fig. 13. Audition designs under the template to find best the placement.

Apply tricot to each block

Tricot stabilizes the shirt fabric while at the same time maintains its softness. Do not be tempted to leave it out. It has the added benefit of supporting any holes or thinning in the fabric that might occur in well-loved shirts. Cut the tricot to the size of the initial cut of your block.

IMPORTANT: When applying the tricot, follow the manufacturer's directions, making sure that the tricot is lying cross-grain to the fabric, which will stabilize the stretchiness properly (Fig. 11).

> **Trish's Tip:** Tricot can be pieced if you want to use up smaller leftover pieces. All the pieces should be going cross-grain to the fabric and overlapped by about 1/8". The tricot yardage requirements given for the quilts are for cutting whole squares, not piecing.

Combining two or more shirts into one block

If you have several shirts with small logos or sayings on them or have a shirt with a front and back with small designs, you can combine them into a single block (Fig. 12).

a) Make the shirt blocks like they would be used whole. Then take the two designs and audition them under the size template you are using to make your blocks. Line everything up so you know it will fit and look nice.

> **Trish's Tip:** Using the templates or any clear ruler that does not have a lot of lines on it allows you to see the designs you are auditioning, making this process much easier (Fig. 13).

b) Measure the size of each piece of the shirt needed when finished and add ¼" to the edges that will be sewn together to allow for a seam allowance. Leave an extra inch or so on all the other sides so the block can be squared up after sewing it together. The designs do not have to be equal in size; they just need to add up to the size of the final block (Fig. 14).

c) Sew the two individual block pieces together (Fig. 15).

d) Square-up the block and trim to its final size (Fig. 16).

> **Trish's Tip:** It is important to cut blocks to their final size *after* any piecing has been done. Sewing knits tends to pull the fabric and cause a warp in the block. Doing the final cutting after sewing gives you a nice straight block to work with.

Modifying tank tops, small shirts, and baby clothes

Items such as tank tops and baby or toddler clothes too small to make a block by themselves can be integrated into a larger block.

Select a blank piece from a T-shirt not being used in the quilt to serve as the background for the smaller items. If you do not have an extra piece of T-shirt, use fabric, another old T-shirt, or buy one the color you want at a thrift shop. Prepare it with tricot.

a) Cut the shoulder seams (Fig. 17).

Fig. 14. Square-up the individual pieces for sewing together.

Fig. 15. Sew the two pieces together.

Fig. 16. Cut the block to its final size.

Fig. 17. Cut the shoulder seams.

Fig. 18a. Cut up the side seams.

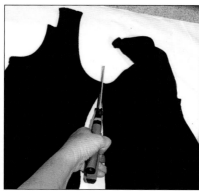

Fig. 18b.

Fig. 19. Place the tank top on the block.

Fig. 20. Cut the tank top to fit the block.

Fig. 21. Appliqué the tank top to the block.

Fig. 22. A toddler's shirt appliquéd to a block

b) Cut up the side seams of the tank top/small shirt (Figs. 18a and b).

c) Place the tank top on top of the prepared background so you can size it appropriately (Fig. 19).

d) Trim the tank top to fit the block (Fig. 20).

e) Fuse the tank top to the background and appliqué in place (Fig. 21).

Trish's Tip: When appliquéing items onto blocks, match the thread as close to the color of the appliqué as possible. Embroidery thread comes in a wide variety of shades, making it easy to match the fabric. Use an open-toe foot to appliqué so that you can see the area you are stitching. The zigzag appliqué stitch should be narrow, about 2.0mm, when going over thin areas and wider, about 4.0mm, when going over thicker areas.

f) Follow the same steps to fit a small child's shirt to a block (Fig. 22).

Modifying shorts or baby/ toddler pants

a) Cut up the right side seam of the shorts or pants (Fig. 23).

b) Cut the crotch seams of the shorts or pants (Fig. 24).

c) Cut up the left side seam of the shorts or pants (Fig. 25).

d) Straighten the center seam so it will lie flat by stitching straight down from the waistband. Trim the seam allowance to ¼" and press open (Fig. 26).

e) Cut open the top edge of the waistband and cut away the elastic and backing fabric to decrease the bulk (Figs. 27 and 28).

f) Apply the fusible to the back of the shorts.

g) Place the shorts in the middle of a background block, making sure the design is within the final cutting dimension. Fuse the shorts to the background and appliqué in place (Fig. 29). See Trish's Tip on page 20.

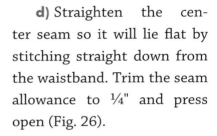

Fig. 23. Cut up the right side seam.

Fig. 24. Cut through the crotch of the pants.

Fig. 25. Cut up the left side seam.

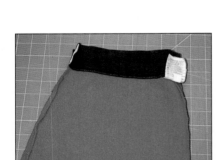

Fig. 26. Straighten the center seam of the shorts and trim the seam.

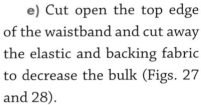

Fig. 27. Cut open the top of the waistband.

Fig. 28. Cut away the elastic and the extra fabric.

Fig. 29. Shorts mounted to the quilt block

Fig. 30. This block is ready to have the missing corners fixed.

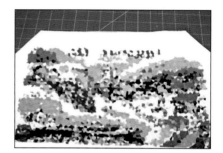

Fig. 31. Cut straight across the corners of the shirt block.

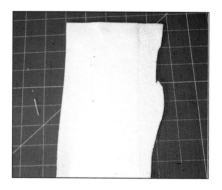

Fig. 32. Cut a straight edge on a shirt scrap.

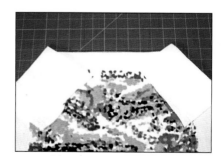

Fig. 33. Line up the straight edges of the block and the scrap pieces of fabric.

Trish's Tip: If any edges of an item you are placing on a block are outside the stitching line, it is not necessary to sew them down as they will be secured when the blocks are put together. Using an appliqué stitch in those areas will only add bulk to the seam allowance.

Adapting slightly smaller shirts to make them the right size or fixing corners of shirts

Sometimes the sleeve areas of shirts are narrow so the cut shirt isn't quite as big as the block size you want. This is easy to fix.

a) Apply tricot to the back of the shirt (Fig. 30).

b) Cut a clean straight edge at the corners (Fig. 31).

c) Fuse tricot onto a scrap piece of fabric from the same shirt that is larger than the area to be fixed. Cut a straight edge on one side of the fabric piece (Fig. 32).

d) Match the straight edges of shirt and prepared scrap pieces. Sew the pieces together with a ¼" seam allowance and press the fabric out (Fig. 33).

e) Place the ruler/template on top of the shirt and trim the corners to the proper size (Fig. 34).

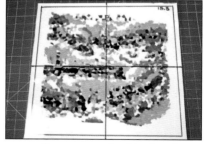

Fig. 34. Square up the block using the template.

Modifying the collars of team jerseys or polo shirts

Shirts with a neckband or collar usually need to be adjusted to make a block.

Team jerseys

a) Follow the initial cutting instructions (page 15).

b) Cut out a portion of the shirt back big enough to fill the hole in the front V-neck, including the neckband. Apply tricot to the "back," which could be either side (Fig. 35).

c) Pin to fill the V-neck of the front of the shirt (Fig. 36).

d) If you are going to use both the back and front of the shirt as blocks, use a portion of a sleeve to fill in the open space using the same process as described above.

e) Sew around the neckline making sure all edges are sewn down close to the edge. This will prevent the neckline from being lifted up by the presser foot during the quilting process (Fig. 37).

f) Square-up the block to the unfinished block size.

Polo Shirts – Keeping the collar on

Follow these directions when the design is high up on the shirt or if you want to keep the collar on the shirt. Before doing any cutting, read this entire section and look at the photos so you know what the end result will look like.

a) Follow the initial cutting instructions (page 14), leaving the collar intact. When separating the front and the back, cut through the collar following in a straight line across from the shoulder seam (Fig. 38).

Fig. 35. Cut off a section of the back.

Fig. 36. Pin the backing piece to the neck.

Fig. 37. Stitch close to the edge of the neckline.

Fig. 38. Polo shirt to be used in a quilt

Fig. 39. Bulky front button area

Fig. 41. Sew the front button area closed.

Fig. 42. Pin the fabric piece in place behind the front of the shirt.

Fig. 40. Cut away the button area to decrease the bulk.

b) Decrease the bulk in the front placket area by cutting the back button section out (Figs. 39 and 40).

c) Reposition the buttonhole section and stitch along the edge of the closure (Fig. 41).

d) Because polo shirts have thick double collars, use the sleeve or part of the back to fill in the neck hole. Apply the tricot to this piece and pin it to the back of the shirt front (Fig. 42).

e) Sew around the neckline with matching thread, making sure all the edges are sewn down close to the edge. This will prevent any pulling or lifting of the collar during the quilting (Fig. 43).

f) Square-up the block to the unfinished block size.

Remove a polo shirt collar.

If the design on the shirt is low on the shirt and you don't need to keep the collar, prepare the shirt like any other T-shirt (Fig. 44).

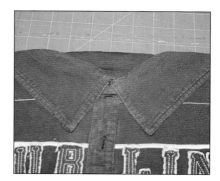

Fig. 43. Stitch the collar down securely.

Fig. 44. Cut the shirt square to eliminate the collar.

Add small designs to the back or the front of the shirt

In this example, there is a small logo on the front of the shirt with the large design on the back (Figs. 45a and b).

Fig. 45a. Front of shirt

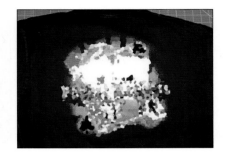

Fig. 45b. Back of shirt

a) Prepare the back of the shirt to the initial squaring-up size.

b) Cut around the small design in the front. Make sure this cut is it at least 1" larger than the finished design to allow room to square it up later.

c) Audition the placement of the small design on the back. In this case, the front logo contains the location of the event, which the back didn't (Fig. 46).

Fig. 46. Audition the placement of the front logo.

d) Apply the fusible to the design from the front while it is at least 1" larger than its final size. Trim the design to its final size, place it on the shirt block where desired. Fuse and appliqué in place (Fig. 47).

Fig. 47. Location of event cut from front and added to the back

Attaching patches and awards to a block

a) Select a piece of the T-shirt that is not being used in the quilt. Make the initial cut of the block and apply tricot.

b) Pin the patches to the prepared block (Fig. 48).

c) Stitch around the patches with matching thread using a straight stitch just inside the outer border or zigzag around the edges, whichever you prefer.

Fig. 48. Patches attached to a large block

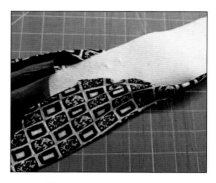

Fig. 49. Remove the stabilizer from the tie.

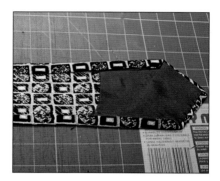

Fig. 50. Trim the fold to ½".

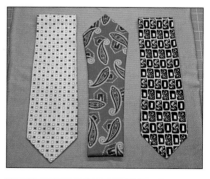

Fig. 51. Tie layout examples

Patches can also be attached to the borders of the quilts. I find it easier to sew them on before the borders are added to the quilt so I have less fabric to move around under the machine, but if you are concerned about placement, you can wait until the top is finished.

Trish's Tip: Add an extra ½" to your border strips as sewing on the patches could pull in the fabric, making the borders uneven. After the patches are sewn on, trim to the correct width and you will have nice straight borders.

Modifying ties for use in a quilt

a) Select a piece of T-shirt fabric as background for the ties. Make the initial cut of the block and apply tricot. Remove any stabilizer from the tie (Fig. 49).

b) Trim the ties leaving a ½" seam allowance from the front folded edge. Removing the stabilizer and trimming the back reduces the bulk and help the ties lie nice and flat (Fig. 50).

c) Apply fusible to the back of the ties.

d) Arrange the ties on the prepared block as desired, making sure the design is within the final cutting dimension (Fig. 51).

e) Cut the final length of the ties only after you have finalized the arrangement.

f) Appliqué the ties in place.

Modifying bags to be used in quilt blocks

a) Select a bag (Fig. 52) and a piece of T-shirt fabric for the background. Make the initial cut of the T-shirt fabric and apply tricot to the back.

b) Cut the handles off the bag and cut down the side and bottom seams (Fig. 53).

c) Cut out the design you want to use from the bag in any shape that you wish—square, rectangular, round, or along the shape of the design itself.

d) Apply the fusible to the back of the bag motif and place on the background, making sure the design is within the final cutting dimension (Fig. 54).

e) Fuse and appliqué in place.

Fig. 52. Cloth shopping bag

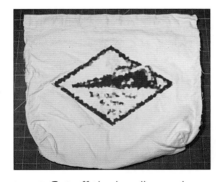

Fig. 53. Cut off the handles and around the bag seam.

Fig. 54. Attach the design to the block.

Modifying hats to be put in quilts

a) Select a piece of T-shirt fabric as background for the design. Make the initial cut and apply tricot to the back.

b) Decide what part of the hat you will be using in your block. In this case the front and the back are going to be used, combined on a single block (Figs. 55a and b).

c) Remove the brim of the hat using a seam ripper (Fig. 56).

Fig. 55a. Parts of the hat that will be used in the block

Fig. 55b.

Fig. 56. Remove the brim of the hat.

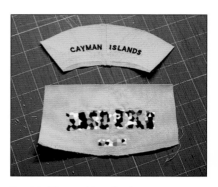

Fig. 57. Shape the designs as desired.

Fig. 58. Arrange on the block and appliqué.

d) Cut around the designs on the hat, front and back, leaving as much fabric as possible.

e) Remove as much extra fabric and stabilizer as possible from the portions of the hat you are using.

Trish's Tip: The more stabilizer you remove from the hat pieces, the better it will lie on the quilt and the easier the quilting process will be.

f) Apply the fusible to the back of the hat designs and cut them to their final shape (Fig. 57).

g) Arrange the hat designs on the block as desired, making sure all the designs are within the final cutting dimension. Appliqué in place (Fig. 58).

Final squaring-up of the blocks

Trim the blocks to the unfinished block size (page 15).

CONGRATULATIONS. You are ready to use these memory blocks in your quilt!

layout and joining

Planning the block layout

a) Look at the initial layout on your Fabric Shopping Guide (page 10). Now is the time to experiment with it if something doesn't look quite right.

b) Once you have an arrangement you like, lay out the blocks on the floor, a table, or design wall following the guide. Scrutinize the final layout. Look at entire blocks including the size and coloring of the design, not just the background color. Most of the time what you have on the small layout will be what you keep. Sometimes, seeing the full-size blocks laid out will suggest changes because a block design, due to color or size, throws off the quilt's balance. Move any blocks you need to in order to achieve the most pleasing overall balance.

c) Take a photo of the layout or write on another paper layout where each block is placed in the final design. Recording the layout now will serve as a placement reminder later if the blocks get mixed up before they are sewn together (Fig. 1).

Fig. 1. Photograph the quilt layout.

Fig. 2a. Pin each row of blocks together, labeling the rows with letters or numbers.

Fig. 2b. Pin and label the rows consecutively all the way down the quilt

Fig. 3. Pin the sashing to the block sides.

Joining the quilt top

This is my favorite method for joining blocks and sashing to make sure I maintain my layout design during the sewing.

Organizing blocks into rows for sewing

a) Stack the blocks by rows horizontally. Start with the top row of the quilt. Move across the row left to right, with the top block in the stack being the far left one in the row and bottom block in the stack being the far right in the row.

b) Pin each row together and label each consecutively beginning with Row 1 or Row A (Figs. 2a and b).

Sewing the rows together

Referring to the final layout or photo to double-check the placement of the blocks, sew the blocks for each row together. Use ¼" seams for all sewing and press away from the blocks throughout.

a) Start with the first block on the left and work your way across the row to the right. Pin the precut lengths of sashing on each side of the first block, right sides together (Fig. 3).

> **Trish's Tip:** Pinning the sashing to the block helps prevent stretching or pulling the fabrics out of shape as you sew them together, resulting in blocks that are square and equal in size.

b) Sew the pinned sashing to opposite sides of the first block. Press (Fig. 4).

c) Pin the second block of the row to the right side sashing of the first block and sew (Fig. 5).

d) Press. Add blocks to the row in order, alternating sashing and blocks as you go, ending with a sashing strip (Fig. 6).

e) Repeat these steps for each row.

> **Trish's Tip:** Keep the label identifying each row attached to the first block in the row to make sure you sew the rows together in proper order later.

Joining the rows

a) Piece the sashing strips that go between the rows with 45-degree angle seams as needed. Overlap the strips at right angles. Pin together and draw a line from the top left corner to the bottom right corner of the overlap. Sew on the line. Trim to ¼" (Fig. 7).

> **Trish's Tip:** Piece your sashing, borders, and binding strips this way. It helps the seams to blend in and not be as noticeable in the final quilt and evenly distributes the extra fullness of the seam allowance. On binding strips, press the seams open.

b) Measure across each row of blocks. They should all be the same length. If there is a difference take the average of the lengths and use this measurement to cut the sashing strips to ensure the quilt rows will be the same size and the quilt even from top to bottom.

c) Pin a sashing strip along the top and bottom of the top row, right sides together. Pin in the middle and at each end, with additional pins along the length of the row, easing any extra fullness where necessary. Sew and press both seams away from the blocks (Fig. 8, page 30).

Fig. 4. Sew the sashing to each side of the block.

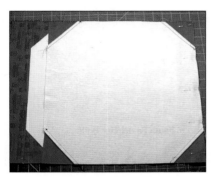

Fig. 5. Pin the second block to the first and sew.

Fig. 6. First row of blocks completed

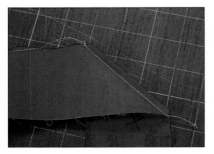

Fig. 7. Stitch sashing strips and trim the seam allowance.

Fig. 8. Sashing sewn to the top and bottom of the top row

Fig. 9. All rows sewn together

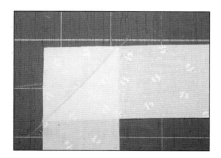

Fig. 10. Draw a 45-degree angle line.

d) Add sashing to the bottom of the second row, pinning as described above. Sew and press as before.

e) Pin the top of second row to the bottom of the top row sashing, again following the technique described above. Sew and press.

f) Follow these steps with the remaining rows (Fig. 9).

Adding the borders

a) Measure across the top and bottom edges of the quilt. Make the border strips this length. If they are not the same length take the average of the two measurements and make the borders this length.

b) To piece strips to get the length you need, overlap the strips at right angles to each other. Draw a 45-degree angle line from top right corner to the bottom left corner of the overlap. Pin in place and sew along the line (Fig. 10).

c) Trim a seam allowance to ¼" and press the seam to one side.

d) Pin the border to the top and bottom edges of the quilt, right sides together, at each end and in the middle first, and then along the length of the border. Sew the border onto the quilt, easing it on as you go.

e) Sew the borders. Press the seams away from quilt.

f) Measure the length of the sides, including the top and bottom borders. If they are not the same length, take the average of the two measurements. Piece strips as needed. Cut the borders to length and add to the sides.

project examples ←————————————————————————————————

Memory quilts come in all shapes and sizes because everyone's memories are different and everyone interprets their memories in different ways. The fun of making them is there really aren't any rules. When deciding what to put in your blocks and how you put them together, anything goes. Many of the seven designs that follow are presented with multiple size options that include everything from wallhangings to full-size quilts.

I don't want you to follow my ideas exactly because they are mine. I want you to think outside the box have fun tailoring the designs to your own style and memories. By using these designs as a springboard you will have an opportunity to incorporate a wide variety of memorabilia into your quilts—T-shirts; neckties; photographs; hats; tote bags; badges; emblems and awards; out-grown baby and toddler clothes; travel souvenirs—any and all can be included.

Browse through the pages ahead as you let the memories and your imagination flow!

I PLAY WITH TRAINS, 70" x 84", made by the author

Easy Memorabilia QUILTS: *ties, t-shirts, photos & more* – Trish Bowman

I PLAY WITH TRAINS – T-SHIRT QUILT

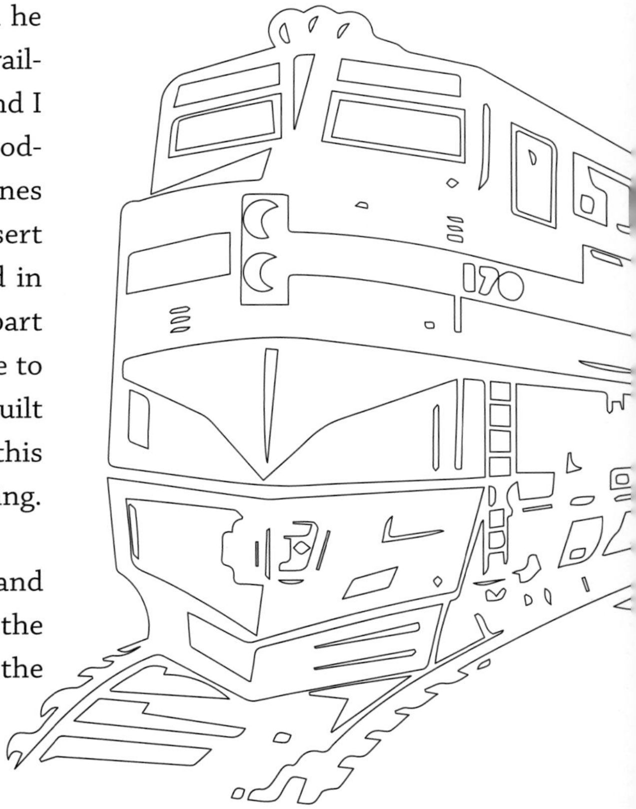

My husband, Doug, received his first train set at age six and he hasn't stopped playing with them since. He had a large model railroad in his parents' basement when we met in high school, and I spent many dates watching him work on it. He has always modeled the Santa Fe railroad with its beautiful Super Chief engines and logos. We have spent time chasing real trains across the desert Southwest and have always had some type of model railroad in every home we have ever lived in. He finally was willing to part with some (but not all!) of his many train shirts and asked me to make a quilt for him. With that request, the design for this quilt was born. Enjoying the use of appliqué to enhance my quilts, this design included the train signals that are a big part of railroading.

While this design is specific to railroading, the basic block and sashing pattern can be used for any theme quilt by omitting the train appliqués. Better yet, design your own appliqués to fit the theme of your quilt!

Fabric Requirements for 12" Finished Blocks

Fabric Needed	12-Shirt Quilt 56" x 70"	16-Shirt Quilt 70" x 70"	20-Shirt Quilt 70" x 84"
Tricot (20" wide)	4⅝ yards	6⅛ yards	7⅝ yards
Sashing	1 yard	1⅓ yards	1½ yards
Corner squares	½ yard	½ yard	⅝ yard
Border	1¾ yards	1⅞ yards	2⅛ yards
Backing	4¾ yards	4¾ yards	5½ yards
Binding	⅔ yard	⅞ yard	1 yard

Cutting Instructions for 12" Finished Blocks

Cutting Instructions	12 Shirts	16 Shirts	20 Shirts
Tricot	(12) 13½" squares	(16) 13½" squares	(20) 13½" squares
Sashing strips	(12) 2½" strips Cut 6 strips into (16) 2½" x 12½".	(15) 2½" strips Cut 7 strips into (20) 2½" x 12½".	(17) 2½" strips Cut 8 strips into (25) 2½" x 12½".
Corner squares	Cut (3) 2½" strips into (48) 2½" x 2½" squares.	Cut (4) 2½" strips into (64) 2½" x 2½" squares.	Cut (5) 2½" strips into (80) 2½" x 2½" squares.
Border	(8) 6½" strips	(9) 6½" strips	(10) 6½" strips
Binding	(7) 2½" strips	(8) 2½" strips	(10) 2½" strips

Fabric Requirements for 13" Finished Blocks

Fabric Needed	12-Shirt Quilt 59"x 74"	16-Shirt Quilt 74" x 74"	20-Shirt Quilt 74" x 89"
Tricot (20" wide)	5 yards	6⅝ yards	8¼ yards
Sashing	1¼ yard	1½ yards	1⅞ yards
Corner squares	½ yard	½ yard	⅝ yard
Border	1¾ yards	1⅞ yards	2⅛ yards
Backing	5⅛ yards	7½ yards	8⅞ yards
Binding	⅞ yard	1 yard	1 yard

Cutting Instructions for 13" Finished Blocks

Cutting Instructions	12 Shirts	16 Shirts	20 Shirts
Tricot	(12) 14½" squares	(16) 14½" squares	(20) 14½" squares
Sashing	(12) 2½" strips Cut 8 strips into (16) 2½" x 13½"	(15) 2½" strips Cut 10 strips into (20) 2½" x 13½"	(23) 2½" strips Cut 13 strips into (25) 2½" x 13½"
Corner squares	Cut (3) 2½" strips into (48) 2½" x 2½" squares.	Cut (4) 2½" strips into (64) 2½" x 2½" squares.	Cut (5) 2½" strips into (80) 2½" x 2½" squares.
Border	(8) 6½" strips	(9) 6½" strips	(10) 6½" strips
Binding	(7) 2½" strips	(8) 2½" strips	(9) 2½" strips

Fabric Requirements for 14" Finished Blocks

Fabric Needed	12-Shirt Quilt 62" x 78"	16-Shirt Quilt 78" x 78"	20-Shirt Quilt 78" x 94"
Tricot (20" wide)	5⅓ yards	7⅛ yards	8¾ yards
Sashing	1⅓ yards	1⅝ yards	1⅞ yards
Corner Squares	⅔ yard	⅞ yard	1⅛ yards
Border	1⅞ yards	2⅛ yards	2⅛ yards
Backing	5⅓ yards	7⅞ yards	9¼ yards
Binding	⅞ yard	1⅛ yards	1⅛ yards

Cutting Instructions for 14" Finished Blocks

Cutting Instructions	12 Shirts	16 Shirts	20 Shirts
Tricot	(12) 15½" squares	(16) 15½" squares	(20) 15½" squares
Sashing	(13) 2½" strips Cut 8 strips into (16) 2½" x 14½".	(16) 2½" strips Cut 10 strips into (20) 2½" x 14½".	(20) 2½" strips Cut 13 strips into (25) 2½" x 14½".
Corner squares	Cut (3) 2½" strips into (48) 2½" x 2½" squares.	Cut (4) 2½" strips into (64) 2½" x 2½" squares.	Cut (5) 2½" strips into (80) 2½" x 2½" squares.
Border	(9) 6½" strips	(10) 6½" strips	(10) 6½" strips
Binding	(8) 2½" strips	(8) 2½" strips	(9) 2½" strips

Fabric Requirements for 15" Finished Blocks

Fabric Needed	12-Shirt Quilt 65" x 82"	16-Shirt Quilt 82" x 82"	20-Shirt Quilt 82" x 99"
Tricot (20" wide)	5⅝ yards	7½ yards	9⅓ yards
Sashing	1⅓ yards	1⅝ yards	1⅞ yards
Corner Squares	⅔ yard	⅞ yard	1⅛ yards
Border	1⅞ yards	2⅛ yards	2¼ yards
Backing	5⅜ yards	8 yards	9½ yards
Binding	⅞ yard	⅞ yard	1 yard

Cutting Instructions for 15" Finished Blocks

Cutting Instructions	12 Shirts	16 Shirts	20 Shirts
Tricot	(12) 16½" squares	(16) 16½" squares	(20) 16½" squares
Sashing	(15) 2½" strips Cut 8 strips into (16) 2½" x 15½".	(19) 2½" strips Cut 10 strips into (20) 2½" x 15½".	(24) 2½" strips Cut 13 strips into (25) 2½" x 15½".
Corners	Cut (3) 2½" strips into (48) 2½" x 2½" squares.	Cut (4) 2½" strips into (64) 2½" x 2½" squares.	Cut (5) 2½" strips into (80) 2½" x 2½" squares.
Border	(9) 6½" strips	(10) 6½" strips	(11) 6½" strips
Binding	(8) 2½" strips	(9) 2½" strips	(10) 2½" strips

Fabric Requirements for Appliqué (optional)

Fabric requirements are the same for all the quilt sizes.

Railroad Crossing Appliqué	
Stitch Witchery or Soft Fuse	½ yard
White	1 fat eighth (9" x 22")
Black	⅛ yard
Red	1 fat eighth (9" x 22")

Train Sign Appliqué	
Stitch Witchery or Soft Fuse	¼ yard
Yellow	1 fat quarter (18" x 22")
Black	⅛ yard

Step 1 – Make the blocks

Follow the directions in Making Memories into Blocks (pages 11–26) to turn your selected shirts and other memorabilia into blocks.

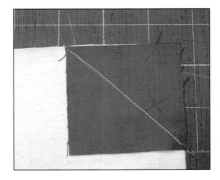

Fig. 1. Stitch on the marked line.

Step 2 – Cut the fabrics

Using the charts pages 33–36, cut the sashing, corner squares, borders, and binding according to the number and size of blocks needed to complete your design.

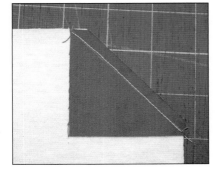

Fig. 2. Trim the seams to ¼".

Step 3 – Add corners to the blocks

a) Draw a diagonal line across the back of (4) 2½" squares.

b) With right sides together, place a marked square in each corner of a block and pin.

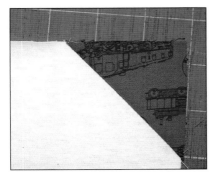

Fig. 3 . Press the fabric out.

c) Stitch on the line (Fig. 1).

d) Trim the seam allowance to ¼" (Fig. 2).

e) Press the seam away from the block (Fig. 3).

f) Repeat for all your blocks.

Step 4 – Plan the block layout (page 27)

Step 5 – Sew the sashing strips and blocks into rows (pages 28–29)

Step 6 – Sew the rows together (pages 29–30)

a) Make the sashing strips to go in between the rows of blocks, piecing the strips as needed.

b) Join the rows of blocks, alternating them with the sashing strips.

Step 7 – Add the border (page 30)

Fig. 4 . Letters are traced for the train sign backwards.

Step 8 – Yellow Railroad Sign Appliqué (optional)

Trish's Tip: Trace all like colors next to each other, such as all the letters, red lights, etc. This allows you to iron the big pieces of fusible onto the fabric and only fussy cut the patterns once.

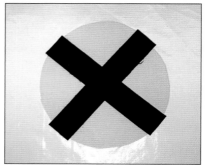

Fig. 5 . Place the crossbars at right angles.

Appliqué Cutting Instructions – yellow RR sign	

Black: sign post
      crossbars
      base
	Cut 1 rectangle 1¼" x 12½".
	Cut 2 rectangles 1½" x 8".
	Cut 1 rectangle 3½" x 4".

Letters	Page 41
Yellow	7½" diameter circle

a) Trace the letters and sign post parts onto the paper side of fusible using a light box. The letters are presented backwards so they will be correct when the letters are fused in place (Fig. 4).

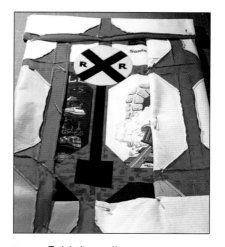

Fig. 6 . Fold the quilt to ease sewing the appliqué.

b) Press the fusible onto the black fabric according to the manufacturer's directions.

c) Cut out the appliqué pieces.

d) Place the 1½" x 8" pieces of black at right angles to each other on top of the yellow circle (Fig. 5, page 38).

e) Trim the edges of the black pieces along the yellow circle so they curve smoothly around the edge of the circle

f) Place the RR letters on the yellow sign and fuse in place. Appliqué the letters and the black cross bars, using a zigzag stitch and matching thread.

g) Place the sign post and base together on an appliqué sheet, overlapping the pieces by ¼". Fuse them together.

h) Apply fusible to the yellow circle, place on top of the post overlapping by ¼", and fuse them together.

i) Pull the completed appliqué off the appliqué sheet, position it on the quilt, and fuse in place.

j) Machine appliqué the sign post onto the quilt (Fig. 6, page 38).

> **Trish's Tips:** Here are a few tips to make appliquéing easier:
>
> **1)** Use thread that matches the appliqué fabric as closely as possible. This helps the stitching disappear into the design rather than take away from it.
>
> **2)** Use your machine's needle down setting if possible as it will make turning the appliqué easier.
>
> **3)** Use an open-toe foot so you can see the area you are stitching well.
>
> **4)** Use a narrow zigzag stitch —about 2.0mm—when going over thin areas and wider— about 4.0mm—when going over thicker areas.

Step 9 - Railroad Crossing Sign Appliqué (optional)

Appliqué Cutting Instructions – RR crossing sign	
Black Fabric – sign post base	Cut 1 rectangle 1" x 16". Cut 1 rectangle 3¼" x 4".
White – RR crossing bars	Cut 2 rectangles 3" x 13"
Letters	See text (page 40).
Red – warning lights	Cut 2 circles 2¾" diameter
Black – warning lights	Cut 2 circles 3½" diameter

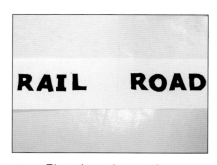

Fig. 7 . Place lettering on the crossbars.

Fig. 8 . Overlap the sign pieces.

Fig. 9 . Attach red circles to the center of the black circles.

a) Trace the letters (page 41) onto the paper side of fusible.

b) Press the fusible with traced patterns onto the appropriate color fabric according to the manufacturer's directions EXCEPT for the black circles and white sign pieces. You will add fusible to these after appliquéing the red circles and letters, respectively.

c) Cut out the appliqué pieces.

d) Position the letters on the white bars. Be sure to leave enough space between "rail" and "road" for the width of the other crossbar. Fuse the letters in place (Fig. 7).

e) Appliqué the letters using a zigzag stitch and matching thread. Press well.

f) Cut the white sign pieces down to 2" x 12" keeping the letters centered.

g) Cut two pieces of fusible 2" x 12" and apply to the white crossbars. Place the pieces at right angles to each other on an appliqué sheet. Fuse the center portion (Fig. 8).

h) Place the crossbars, sign post, and base on an appliqué sheet, overlapping the pieces by ¼". Fuse together.

i) Make the warning lights. Apply fusible to the red circles and fuse them to the center of the black circles (Fig. 9). Zigzag stitch around the red part of the light using matching thread. Apply fusible to the backs of the black circles.

j) On the appliqué sheet, place the lights on either side of the signpost just under the crossing sign. Overlap the inner edges of the lights with the post by ¼".

k) Pull the completed appliqué off the appliqué sheet and position it on the quilt. Fuse in place (Fig. 10).

l) Appliqué in place.

Your quilt top is complete!

Step 10 - Finishing

a) See Don't Forget the Back (pages 88–90).

b) Quilt as desired.

c) Add binding and a sleeve (pages 91–93).

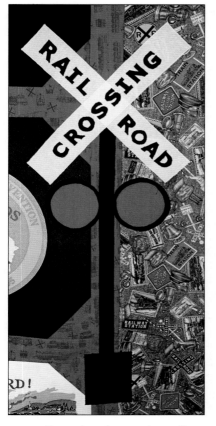

Fig. 10. Fuse the sign to the quilt top.

RAIL ROAD CROSSING RR

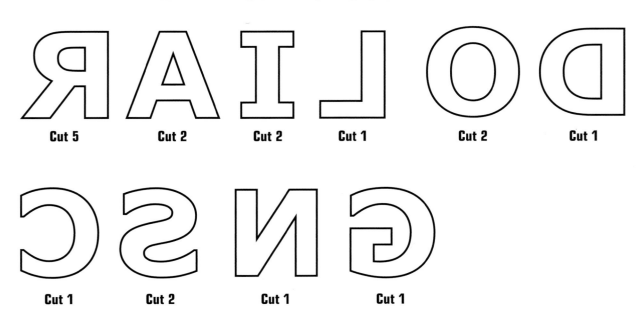

Cut 5   Cut 2   Cut 2   Cut 1   Cut 2   Cut 1

Cut 1   Cut 2   Cut 1   Cut 1

REACH FOR THE STARS, 66" x 66", made by the author

Easy Memorabilia QUILTS: *ties, t-shirts, photos & more* – Trish Bowman

REACH FOR THE STARS – T-SHIRT AND PANEL QUILT

My husband and I are big space enthusiasts from way back. We even spent part of our honeymoon touring the Kennedy Space Center. Our children got the bug from us and took it a step further, with Christopher going to Space Camp at the Kennedy Space Center in Florida and both of them going to the U.S. Space & Rocket Center in Alabama. Christopher did the Aviation Challenge and Jennifer went to Space Camp.

We always watched the shuttle launches on television and were excited when we moved to central Florida and could watch them in person. We were able to go out to the coast for several but watched many, including the spectacular night launches, from our back yard. It was always awe-inspiring. When they decided to retire the shuttle I decided to make all of us memory quilts of the experiences. I found a space panel and fabric, which I loved, and then went online and got shirts representing the launches we saw in person and others that brought back all the wonderful memories we have from that fantastic era.

This quilt integrates fabric panels and smaller squares containing embroideries and other items. The project also offers different sizes of blocks. This design can be used to make any size and theme of quilt.

If you want to do the basic quilt just using the star borders, follow the fabric directions for the appropriate block and quilt size (see pages 46–49). If you want to make a quilt using fabric panels, refer to the directions for REACH FOR THE STARS (page 44).

Fabric Requirements for REACH FOR THE STARS, a 9-Block Quilt with Fabric Panels

Fabric Needed	Yardage
Tricot (20" width) for the T-shirt blocks	2¼ yards
Frame Borders for panel squares – 2 complementary fabrics	Inner frames ½ yard Outer frames ⅝ yard
Frame border for shirt blocks	½ yard
Sashing	1⅛ yards
Stars	1 yard
Inner border	⅔ yard
Outer border	2 yards
Backing	7⅞ yards
Binding	⅞ yard

Cutting Instructions for REACH FOR THE STARS, a 9-Block Quilt with Fabric Panels

	Cutting Instructions
Tricot	Cut squares the size required by your shirt designs.
Frames around panel blocks, as required. (Adjust for the number of panel blocks you have)	Inner frame 5 strips 2½" wide Outer frame 8 strips 2½" wide
Frames around shirt blocks as required.	8 strips 1" wide
Sashing	11 strips 2½" wide
# sashing pieces	20 strips 2½" x 14½" 4 strips 2½" x 16"
Stars	10 strips 2½" wide
# squares for star centers and points	148 squares 2½" x 2½"
Inner border	7 strips 2½" wide
Outer border	8 strips 6¼" wide 2 strips 2½" wide
Binding	8 strips 2½" wide

Step 1 — Making the blocks

Evaluate your panel and the shirts you want to use to determine the design size. Measure whichever panel section or shirt design is the biggest to determine the size of all the blocks. In my case, the T-shirts had the biggest designs, so I made those blocks first. Once they were sized correctly, I framed the fabric panel blocks so they would be the same size. If your fabric panels are bigger, you would do this in reverse.

The object is to add as many borders as needed to smaller individual blocks, whether they are T-shirt blocks or panel blocks in order to make them all the same size.

a) Using coordinating fabrics, add frames to the blocks as necessary. I added two framing borders to each panel block in REACH FOR THE STARS (Fig. 1).

b) Check the measurements of all your panel blocks, trimming to the final size as required.

Fig. 1 . Framed block

Fabric and Cuttings for Block-Size Variations of REACH FOR THE STARS without Panel Blocks

Fabric Requirements for 12" x 12" Finished Blocks

Fabric Needed	9-Block Quilt 60" x 60"	12-Block Quilt 60" x 74"	16-Block Quilt 74" x 74"
Tricot (20" width)	3¾ yards	4⅞ yards	6½ yards
Sashing	⅞ yard	1⅛ yards	1¼ yards
Stars	1 yard	1⅛ yards	1⅜ yards
Inner border	⅔ yard	⅔ yard	⅔ yard
Outer border	2 yards	2 yards	2⅛ yards
Backing	4¼ yards	5 yards	7½ yards
Binding	⅔ yard	⅔ yard	⅞ yard

Cutting Instructions for 12" x 12" finished blocks

Cutting Instructions	9 Blocks	12 Blocks	16 Blocks
Tricot	(9) 13½" squares	(12) 13½" squares	(16) 13½" squares
Sashing	(9) 2½" strips	(11) 2½" strips	(14) 2½" strips
# sashing pieces	(24) 2½" x 12½"	(31) 2½" x 12½"	(40) 2½" x 12½"
Stars	(10) 2½" strips	(12) 2½" strips	(14) 2½" strips
# squares for star centers	(20) 2½" x 2½"	(24) 2½" x 2½"	(29) 2½" x 2½"
# squares for star points	(128) 2½" x 2½"	(156) 2½" x 2½"	(192) 2½" x 2½"
Inner border	(6) 2½" strips	(6) 2½" strips	(7) 2½" strips
Outer border	(8) 6¼" strips (2) 2½" strips	(8) 6¼" strips (2) 2½" strips	(9) 6¼" strips (2) 2½" strips
Binding	(7) 2½" strips	(7) 2½" strips	(8) 2½" strips

Fabric Requirements for 13" x 13" Finished Blocks

Fabric Needed	9-Block Quilt 63" x 63"	12-Block Quilt 63" x 78"	16-Block Quilt 78" x 78"
Tricot (20" width)	3¾ yards	4⅞ yards	½ yard
Sashing	1 yard	1⅛ yards	1⅜ yards
Stars	1 yard	1⅛ yards	1⅜ yards
Inner border	⅔ yard	⅞ yard	⅞ yard
Outer border	2 yards	2⅛ yards	2¼ yards
Backing	4⅓ yards	5¼ yards	7¾ yards
Binding	⅔ yard	⅞ yard	⅞ yard

Cutting Instructions for 13" x 13" Finished Blocks

Cutting Instructions	9 Blocks	12 Blocks	16 Blocks
Tricot	(9) 14½" square	(12) 14½" square	(16) 14½" square
Sashing	Cut (10) 2½" strips into (24) 2½" x 13½" pieces.	Cut (12) 2½" strips into (31) 2½" x 13½" pieces.	Cut (15) 2½" strips into (40) 2½" x 13½" pieces.
Star centers and points	Cut (10) 2½" strips into (148) 2½" x 2½" squares.	Cut (12) 2½" strips into (180) 2½" x 2½" squares.	Cut (14) 2½" strips into (221) 2½" x 2½" squares.
Inner border	(6) 2½" strips	(7) 2½" strips	(8) 2½" strips
Outer border	(8) 6¼" strips (2) 2½" strips	(8) 6¼" strips (2) 2½" strips	(9) 6¼" strips (2) 2½" strips
Binding	(8) 2½" strips	(9) 2½" strips	(10) 2½" strips

Fabric Requirements for 14" x 14" Finished Blocks

Fabric Needed	9-Block Quilt 66" x 66"	12-Block Quilt 66" x 82"	16-Block Quilt 82" x 82"
Tricot (20" width)	4⅜ yards	5⅔ yards	7½ yards
Sashing	1 yard	1¼ yards	1⅜ yards
Stars	1 yard	1⅛ yards	1⅜ yards
Inner border	⅔ yard	⅔ yard	⅞ yard
Outer border	2 yards	2⅛ yards	2¼ yards
Backing	4½ yards	5⅜ yards	8 yards
Binding	⅔ yard	⅞ yard	⅞ yard

Cutting Instructions for 14" x 14" Finished Blocks

Cutting Instructions	9 Blocks	12 Blocks	16 Blocks
Tricot	(9) 15½" squares	(12) 15½" squares	(16) 15½" squares
Sashing	Cut (10) 2½" strips into (24) 2½" x 14½" pieces.	Cut (13) 2½" strips into (31) 2½" x 14½" pieces.	Cut (16) 2½" strips into (40) 2½" x 14½" pieces.
Star centers and points	Cut (10) 2½" strips into (148) 2½" x 2½" squares.	Cut (12) 2½" strips into (180) 2½" x 2½" squares.	Cut (14) 2½" strips into (221) 2½" x 2½" squares.
Inner border	(6) 2½" strips	(7) 2½" strips	(8) 2½" strips
Outer border	(8) 6¼" strips (2) 2½" strips	(9) 6¼" strips (2) 2½" strips	(10) 6¼" strips (2) 2½" strips
Binding	(7) 2½" strips	(8) 2½" strips	(9) 2½" strips

Step 2 – Cut the fabrics

Using the charts (pages 46–49), cut the sashing, corners, star components, borders, and binding according to the number and size of blocks needed to complete your design.

Fabric Requirements for 15" x 15" Finished Blocks

Fabric Needed	9-Block Quilt 69" x 69"	12-Block Quilt 69" x 86"	16-Block Quilt 86" x 86"
Tricot (20" width)	4½ yards	6 yards	8⅛ yards
Sashing	1⅛ yards	1¼ yards	1½ yards
Stars	1 yard	1⅛ yards	1⅜ yards
Inner border	⅔ yard	⅞ yard	⅞ yard
Outer border	2⅛ yards	2⅛ yards	2¼ yards
Backing	4¾ yards	5⅔ yards	7½ yards
Binding	⅔ yard	⅞ yard	1 yard

Cutting Instructions for 15" x 15" Finished Blocks

Cutting Instructions	9 Blocks	12 Blocks	16 Blocks
Tricot	(9) 16½" squares	(12) 16½" squares	(16) 16½" squares
Sashing	Cut (12) 2½" strips into (24) 2½" x 15½" pieces.	Cut (14) 2½" strips into (31) 2½" x 15½" pieces.	Cut (17) 2½" strips into (40) 2½" x 15½" pieces.
Star centers and points	Cut (10) 2½" strips into (148) 2½" x 2½" squares.	Cut (12) 2½" strips into (180) 2½" x 2½" squares.	Cut (14) 2½" strips into (221) 2½" x 2½" squares.
Inner border	(7) 2½" strips	(8) 2½" strips	(9) 2½" strips
Outer border	(9) 6¼" strips (2) 2½" strips	(10) 6¼" strips (2) 2½" strips	(10) 6¼" strips (2) 2½" strips
Binding	(7) 2½" strips	(8) 2½" strips	(9) 2½" strips

Step 3 – Make the star sashing

a) Fold a 2½" star fabric square in half and finger press a seam down the middle.

b) Place the square on one end of a precut sashing strip, right sides together, with the fold running the length of the strip (Fig. 2, page 50).

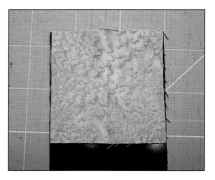

Fig. 2. Place a finger-pressed star square on the sashing piece.

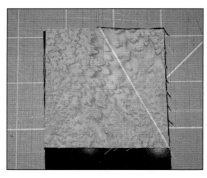

Fig. 3. Draw a stitching guideline.

Figs. 4a and b . Trim the seam to ¼". Press the fabric out.

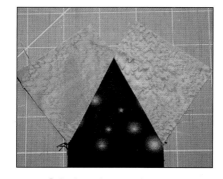

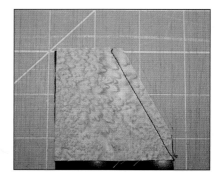

Fig. 5. Prepare a second square for stitching.

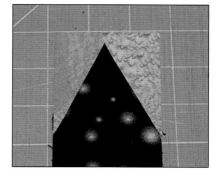

Fig. 6. Stitch, trim, and press the second square.

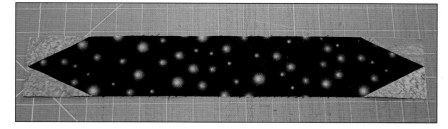

Fig. 7. Finished end of sashing strip

Fig. 8. Completed sashing strip

c) Using a ruler, draw a stitching guideline from the top center (the fold) to the bottom right corner of the square (Fig. 3).

d) Stitch on the line. Trim the seam allowance to ¼" and press the seam out (Figs. 4a and b).

e) Repeat with a second square, drawing the stitching guideline from the top center to the bottom left corner (Fig. 5).

f) Stitch, trim the seam allowance, and press as before (Fig. 6).

g) Trim the star fabric to match the original shape of the sashing strip. Be sure to leave ¼" seam allowance of star fabric at the point created on the sashing strip (Fig. 7).

h) Repeat steps a through g on the other end of the sashing strip and for the remaining sashing strips (Fig. 8).

Step 4– Join the blocks and sashing units

a) Lay out rows of your blocks, alternating them with sashing strips, starting and ending with a sashing strip. Join the strips and blocks into rows (Fig. 9).

Fig. 9. Completed row

b) Make sashing rows of alternating 2½" star fabric squares and sashing strips, using as many strips as the number of blocks in your rows. Press the seams toward the squares. Make one more sashing row than the number of block rows for your quilt (Fig. 10).

Fig. 10. Sashing row

c) Position the sashing rows between the rows of blocks. Sew the rows together.

Step 5– Add the inner and outer borders (page 30)

a) Add the inner border.

b) To continue the star theme used in the sashing, make a Star block for each corner of the outer border. Cut the 2½" wide border strips into 32 squares 2½" x 2½".

c) Using a 2½" square of border fabric and 2 squares of star point fabric, repeat steps a–f for making the sashing star points (pages 49–50). Trim the star point unit to measure 2½" x 2½" (Fig. 11).

Fig. 11. Border star point unit. Make 16.

Fig. 12. Completed corner block. Make 4.

d) For each corner Star block, lay out 4 star point units, 1 star fabric square, and 4 outer border squares as shown (Fig. 12).

e) Join the squares and star point units into rows, then sew the rows together.

f) Measure and cut both the side and top and bottom outer borders. Piece as necessary for the needed length.

g) Add the side borders to the quilt top.

h) Add the corner Star blocks to both ends of the top and bottom border strips. Add to the quilt top.

Your quilt top is completed!

Step 6 - Finishing

a) See Don't Forget the Back (pages 88–90).

b) Quilt as desired.

c) Add binding and a sleeve (pages 91–93).

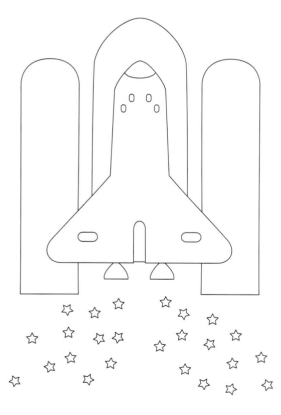

SAILING THE OCEAN BLUE, 64" x 80", made by the author

SAILING THE OCEAN BLUE – T-SHIRT QUILT WITH OPTIONAL PIECED BLOCKS

My husband and I love to travel and see new things. We rarely go to the same place twice because there is just too much in the world we want to see. Our bucket list just says, "Everything." We went on our first cruise over 30 years ago and caught the bug. In the last 10 years, with the kids grown and our lives a little more flexible, we have been able to go on more. We love the ability to travel without having to pack and unpack. We adore snorkeling so have been going to more places where we can do that. The best thing about cruising is the isolation. The phones get put in the safe and we don't do Internet while on the ship. It is wonderful.

This quilt shows how you can integrate optional pieced blocks into your quilt to enhance your design and bring all your memories together. When we travel, including cruising, I, like any other fabricaholic, try to find quilt shops and buy fabric. I look for fabrics from the area. In this quilt I used fabric I bought on our travels in Alaska and the Caribbean.

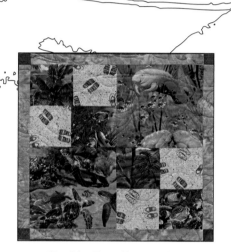

Fig. 1. Double Four-Patch block

Fabric Requirements for a 12-Block 64" x 80" Quilt

Fabric Needed	Yardage
Tricot (20" width)	5⅔ yards
Light blue for sashing	⅔ yard
Dark blue for sashing	⅔ yard
Inner border	½ yard
Outer border	1⅞ yards
Backing	5 yards
Binding	⅝ yard
Assorted fabrics for optional pieced blocks	⅔ yard total

Cutting Instructions

	Cutting Instructions
Tricot	12 squares 15½" x 15½"
Assorted fabrics for optional pieced blocks	8 squares 4" x 4" and 2 squares 7½" x 7½" for each block
Light blue sashing	14 strips 1½" wide
Dark blue sashing	14 strips 1½" wide
Inner border	7 strips 1½" wide
Outer border	9 strips 6½" wide
Binding	8 strips 2½" wide

Step 1 – Make the blocks (pages 11–26)

a) Follow the directions in Making Memories into Blocks (pages 11–26) to turn your selected shirts and other memorabilia into blocks.

b) Piece optional Double Four-Patch blocks with 2 four-patch units (made with 8 squares 4" x 4" each) and 2 squares 7½" x 7½" cut from assorted fabrics (Fig. 1, page 54).

c) Trim all blocks to measure 14½" x 14½".

Step 2 – Cut the fabrics

Using the chart above, cut the sashing, borders, and binding.

Step 3 – Plan the block layout (page 27)

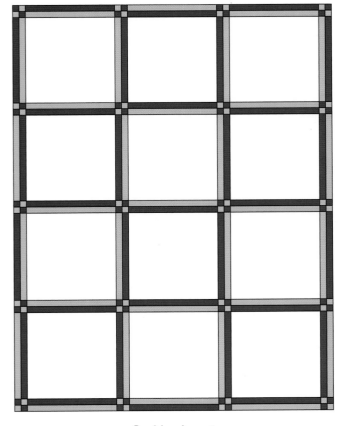

Sashing layout

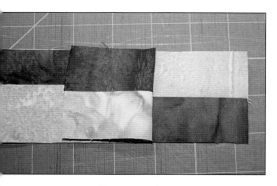

Fig. 2. Position the strip-sets for cutting.

Fig. 3. Cut 20 pairs.

Fig. 4. Make 20.

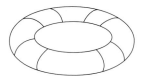

Step 4 – Make the sashing

a) Make 14 strip-sets with the 1½" light and dark blue sashing strips. Press toward the dark blue.

b) Place 2 strip-sets right sides together, positioning the light blue strips opposite each other—one strip-set with light fabric on top and one with dark fabric on top (Fig. 2).

c) Cut 20 segment pairs 1½" wide (Fig. 3).

d) Sew segment pairs together to create Four-Patch blocks. Press the seams open (Fig. 4).

e) Cut 31 segments 14½" long from the remaining sashing strip-sets.

Step 5– Join the blocks and sashing units

a) Refer to your layout to arrange the blocks and sashing strips in rows.

IMPORTANT – Make sure to alternate the position of the light and dark blue from block to block and from row to row. Refer to the sashing layout diagram (page 55).

b) Sew the sashing units and blocks into rows (Fig. 5).

c) Make 5 rows of 3 sashing strips and 4 Four-Patch blocks each. Pay close attention to the position of the light and dark blues (Fig. 6).

d) Position the sashing rows between the rows of blocks. The top, middle, and bottom rows are positioned as shown in figure 7. Turn the second and fourth rows 180 degrees. Refer again to the sashing layout diagram (page 55).

e) Join the block and sashing rows, matching the seams.

Fig. 5. The first two rows with sashing

Fig. 6. Make 5.

Step 6 – Add the inner and outer borders (page 30)

Your quilt top is complete!

Step 7 - Finishing

a) See Don't Forget the Back (pages 88–90).

b) Quilt as desired.

c) Add binding and a sleeve (pages 91–93).

Fig. 7. All the rows sewn together.

DIVIDED BY SERVICE, UNITED BY LOVE, 77" x 97", made by the author
DIVIDED BY SERVICE, UNITED BY LOVE ©Trish Bowman

Easy Memorabilia QUILTS: *ties, t-shirts, photos & more* – Trish Bowman

DIVIDED BY SERVICE, UNITED BY LOVE –
THEME QUILT

Our families have always been very patriotic. Doug's dad served in the Army while Doug was growing up and my dad had been in the Navy before he was married. When Doug and I started dating, he took me to my first Army/Navy football game. When he picked me up at my house that morning I had every intention of rooting for Navy, even though I was going with a bunch of Army people. Well, we got to Doug's house to meet up with his dad and Doug went and got the mail. His acceptance to West Point was there. Needless to say, I called my dad and told him I was sorry but I was now rooting for Army! He laughed and the fun began.

Every year after that was "war." We pulled all kinds of pranks on each other but it was all done with love and respect. If you have ever gone to an Army/Navy game, one of the longest running college football rivalries in the country, you will understand there is nothing like it in the world. You have to experience it just once to get it.

About 20 years ago our nephew was accepted to the Air Force Academy. I don't know where we went wrong influencing him but we love him anyway! I came up with the saying "Divided by service, united by love" and put it on sweatshirts for the family to wear with Army, Navy, and Air Force written on it. It really spoke about our feelings for the services and us. We love and respect each other but there will always be that friendly rivalry between the services and, therefore, us.

I designed this quilt for all the families out there who have families in the service. It is meant to be a family military history quilt that you can add to over the years as your family's life of service continues. I am proud of the men and women who have fought for our freedoms and have thought of them a lot over these months of writing this book. If it weren't for them I wouldn't have the right to write it in the first place. God bless them all.

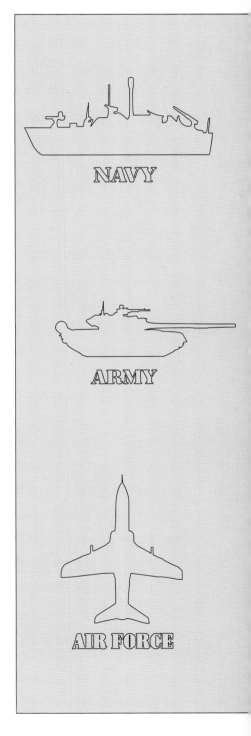

NAVY

ARMY

AIR FORCE

Fabric Requirements

Fabric Needed	Yardage
Army (Center Section)	2¾ yards
Navy (Top Section)	1⅞ yards
Air Force (Bottom Section)	1⅞ yards
Red (divider squares)	½ yard
Black (letter appliqués)	⅓ yard
Inner border	⅞ yard
Middle border	⅞ yard
Outer border	2¼ yards
Backing	8¾ yards
Binding	1 yard
Paper-backed fusible for letter appliqués	⅓ yard SoftFuse

Cutting Instructions

Fabric Needed	Cutting Instructions
Army	Cut 6 strips 10½" wide into 8 segments: (2)10½", (2) 20½", and (4) 30½" long Cut 2 strips 5½" wide into 10 squares 5½" x 5½". Cut 2 strips 3" wide.
Navy	Cut 3 strips 10½" wide into 4 segments: 10½", 20½" 30½", and 40½" long. Cut 1 strip 5½" wide into 5 squares 5½" x 5½". Cut 1 strip 3" wide.
Air Force	Cut 3 strips 10½" wide into 4 segments: 10½", 20½", 30½", and 40½" long. Cut 1 strip 5½" wide into 5 squares 5½" x 5½". Cut 1 strip 3" wide.
Red (four-patch units)	Cut 4 strips 3" wide.
Inner border	Cut 6 strips 2" wide.
Middle border	Cut 6 strips 1½" wide.
Outer border	10 strips 6½" wide. (See Trish's Tip page 61)
Binding	9 strips 2½" wide.

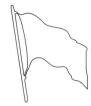

Trish's Tip: If you are concerned about appliqué bunching the outer border fabric, cut 4 of these strips wider and then cut them down after the appliqué is finished.

Step 1 – Cut the fabrics

Using the chart on page 60, cut the theme fabrics, four-patch unit strips, borders, and binding.

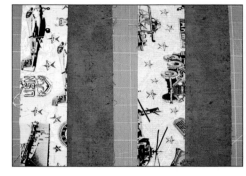

Fig. 1. Navy (left) and Army (right) strip-sets.

Step 2 – Make Navy/Army pieced blocks

a) Make a strip-set with 3" strips of Navy and red. Make a second strip-set with 3" strips of Army and red. Press the seams towards the dark fabric (Fig. 1).

b) Place the 2 strip-sets on your cutting mat, right sides together, with the red fabrics opposite each other (Fig. 2).

c) Cut 10 segment sets 3" wide.

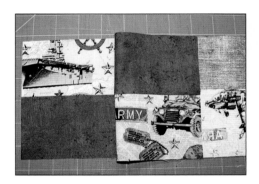

Fig. 2. Position the strip-sets for cutting.

Trish's Tip: Cutting the sets this way puts them together to be sewn in the next step.

d) Sew the sets together using a ¼" seam allowance. Press the seam to the side (Fig. 3).

e) Sew 5 Navy/Army four-patch units to the 5½" Navy fabric squares, with the Navy fabrics touching. Sew 5 Navy/Army four-patch units to the 5½" Army squares with the Army fabrics touching. Make sure the larger squares are oriented correctly. (The

Fig. 3. Make 10 Army/Navy four-patch units.

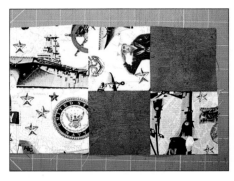

Fig. 4. Match the service fabrics.

Fig. 5. Sew Army and Navy sets together and press. Make 5.

orientation of the four-patch squares is not as important.) Press the seam toward the larger squares (Fig. 4).

f) Position the units as shown and sew together (Fig. 5).

Step 3 – Make Air Force/Army pieced blocks

These blocks are made just like the Army/Navy blocks, but feature Air Force fabric instead of Navy.

a) Make a strip-set with 3" strips of Air Force and red. Make a second strip-set with 3" strips of Army and red. Press the seams towards the dark fabric.

b) Place the strip-sets right sides together and cut 10 segment sets 3" wide. Join into 10 four-patch units.

c) Join the four-patch units with the matching 5½" squares as before (Fig. 6).

d) Position the units as shown and sew together (Fig. 7).

Fig. 6. Match the service fabrics.

Fig. 7. Sew Army and Air Force sets together and press. Make 5.

Step 4 – Join the blocks

a) Lay out the pieced blocks and 10½" wide segments of Army, Navy, and Air Force fabrics according to the quilt layout diagram (page 64). Be sure to match up the service fabrics.

b) Join the blocks and segments into rows.

c) Join the rows together.

Step 5 – Add the inner and middle borders (page 30)

Step 6 – Make the letter appliqués

a) Make templates of the letters (pages 65–67) needed to spell out "divided by service united by love."

b) Place the templates onto paper-backed fusible and trace the number of letters indicated.

c) Press the fusible onto the back of the black fabric. Cut out the letters.

Step 7 – Add the outer border

a) Piece the border strips as needed. Cut the side borders to length. Add to the quilt top.

b) Piece 2 border strips each for the top and bottom borders.

c) Center "divided by service" left-to-right and up-and-down on the top border.

d) Fuse the letters onto the border, then machine appliqué them in place. Use a narrow zigzag stitch with matching thread.

e) Repeat steps c & d to appliqué "united by love" on the bottom border.

f) Cut the borders to size, making sure to keep the letters centered. Trim the width to 6½" if you cut the border strips wider than needed, again, making sure the letters are centered.

g) Attach the top and bottom borders to the quilt making sure the border sayings are facing in the right direction before sewing them on. Refer to the quilt photo (page 58).

Step 8 - Finishing

a) See Don't Forget the Back (pages 88–90).

b) Quilt as desired. I quilted this quilt before putting the names on, as this is a memory quilt meant to be added to over the years. I didn't want some of the names quilted on and others not.

c) Add binding and a sleeve (pages 91–93).

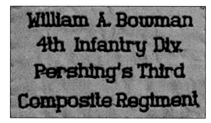

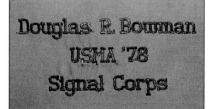

Fig. 8. Name patch examples

Step 9 – Placing names on the quilt

a) Make a list of all family members who have served in the military. This can be as simple as just their name or you can choose to include branch, unit, dates of service, or anything you feel is important to that person's service.

b) Embroider or write the information you gathered on a piece of fabric. Create one patch per person. The example on the upper left is one I made for my husband's grandfather, who served in World War I, already sewn onto the quilt. The one on the lower left is my husband's prior to completion. They are both simple embroideries on brown fabric.

c) Hand sew the patches onto the quilt, matching the service branch with the fabric. Your quilt is done, at least until you have another service member to add to it!

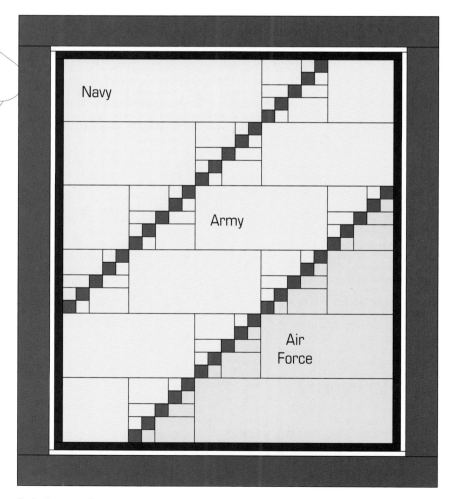

Quilt layout diagram

Appliqué letters for outer border:
DIVIDED BY SERVICE, UNITED BY LOVE ©Trish Bowman

These letters are to be traced onto fusible, using a light box, so when ironed on fabric and cut they will be correct.

Cut 4

Cut 4

Cut 3

Cut 5

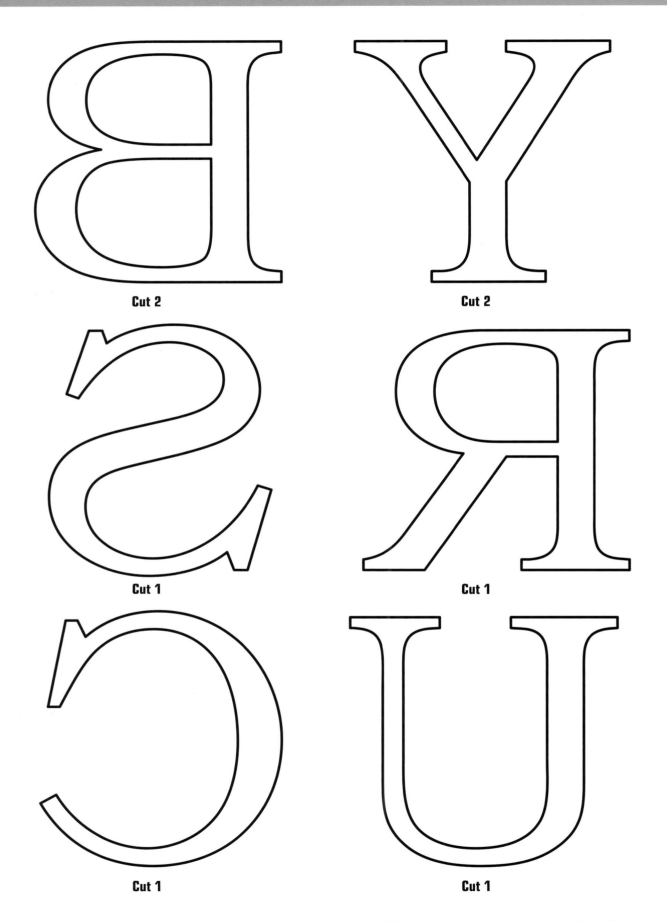

Cut 2

Cut 2

Cut 1

Cut 1

Cut 1

Cut 1

Appliqué letters for outer border:
DIVIDED BY SERVICE, UNITED BY LOVE ©Trish Bowman

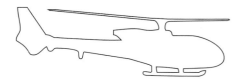

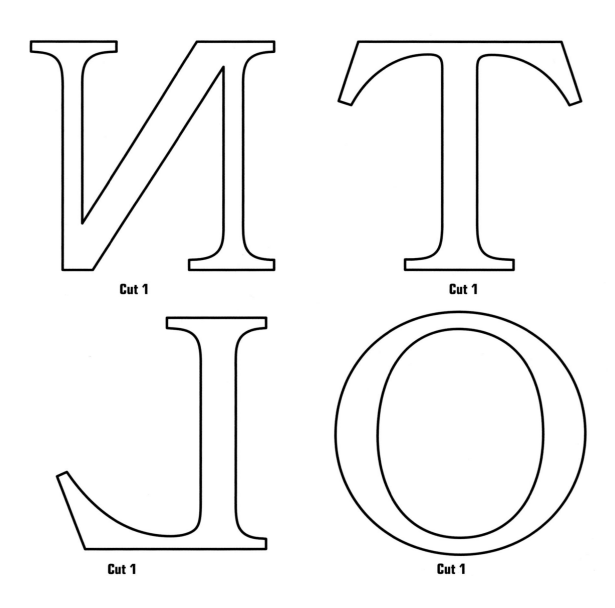

Cut 1

Cut 1

Cut 1

Cut 1

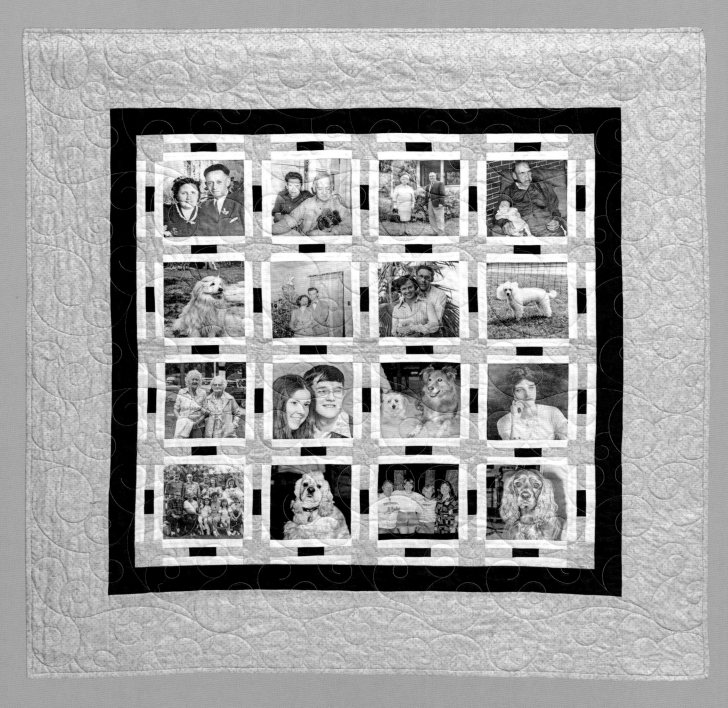

THOSE WERE THE DAYS, 50" x 50", made by the author

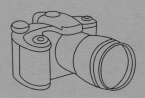

THOSE WERE THE DAYS – PHOTO QUILT

We all have so many wonderful memories that get shoved back in our minds with our busy lives, yet when you see a photo they all come flooding back as if they happened only hours or days ago. My house is full of photos and I would have more if I only had the space. Photo quilts are a great way to remember a special time in your life or to help that special someone remember theirs.

These quilts can be of a single event or cover a span of years. Like all quilts there is no right or wrong; just go with a theme or a feeling. For my version, presented here, I wanted to include relatives, past and present, that have impacted my husband's and my life plus our precious puppies that have meant and still mean so much to us.

Enjoy going through your photos and making your own memories come to life. You just may end up with more than one quilt!

Fabric Requirements for a 16-Block Quilt

Fabric Needed	Yardage
Photo fabric	2 packages / 16+ pieces
Gold	⅔ yard
Brown	1⅛ yards
White	⅞ yard
Inner border	⅝ yard
Outer border	1⅝ yards
Backing	3⅔ yards
Binding	⅔ yard

Cutting Instructions

	Cutting Instructions
Gold	Cut 6 strips 2½" wide Cut 2 of the strips into (25) 2½" x 2½" squares.
Brown	Cut 2 strips 2½" wide.
White	Cut 14 strips 1³⁄₁₆" wide into 80 pieces 6½" long.*
Inner border	Cut 5 strips 2½" wide.
Outer border	Cut 7 strips 6½" wide.
Binding	Cut 6 strips 2½" wide.

* Trish's Tip: When doing odd measurements like this, it is helpful to use masking tape to mark the measurement on your ruler. Doing this makes it easier to quickly find the same point when doing multiple cuts.

Step 1 – Make the blocks

a) Gather the photos you would like to put into your quilt.

b) Using your computer, scanner, and whatever photo program you have, prepare the photos so that they can be printed on fabric. I use Printed Treasures® fabric sheets, which work well with my ink jet printer, but you can use any product designed for this purpose.

This step is your opportunity to crop and modify the pictures so that they fit your theme. In my case, the originals were sized to fill the finished block (6" square) and colorized in sepia tone to give them an old-fashioned feeling (Fig. 1).

c) Follow the manufacturer's directions and print the photos on the fabric.

Fig. 1. Photo square ready for the quilt.

d) Cut each printed photo to measure 6½" x 6½".

e) If any of your photos do not come out the right size or shape, there will be some white fabric showing within the photo square. I added brown fabric to the top and bottom of one of my photo squares to hide the white and blend the square into the quilt.

Fig. 2. Add fabric to bring the photo to the right block size.

f) Cut a complementary fabric 1" wider and longer than the area needed to be covered. With right sides together, place the fabric on the photo square and sew along the picture's edge to eliminate all the white, then press. Cut the modified photo square to measure 6½" x 6½" (Fig. 2).

Step 2 – Cut the fabrics

Using the charts on pages 69–70, cut the sashing, borders, and binding.

Fig. 3. Make 2 strip-sets.

Step 3 – Plan the block layout (page 27)

Step 4 – Make the sashing

a) Make 2 strip-sets with 1 brown and 2 gold 2½" strips each. Press the seams toward the dark fabric. Check that the strip-sets measure 6½" wide (Fig. 3).

b) Cut 40 segments 1³⁄₁₆" wide.

c) Sew a 1³⁄₁₆" x 6½" white strip to both sides of the gold-and-white segments. Press toward the white strips (Fig. 4).

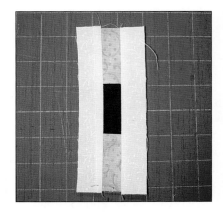

Fig. 4. Make 40 sashing units.

d) Join 4 sashing units and 5 gold 2½" x 2½" squares into sashing rows (Fig. 5, page 72).

Fig. 5. Make 5 rows of alternate squares and sashing units.

Step 5 – Join the blocks (pages 28–30)

a) Referring to your quilt layout plan, make 4 rows of blocks and 5 sashing units.

b) Join the block rows with the sashing rows (Fig. 6).

Step 6 – Add the inner and outer borders (page 30)

Your quilt top is complete!

Step 7 – Finishing

a) See Don't Forget the Back (pages 88–90).

b) Quilt as desired.

c) Add binding and a sleeve (pages 91–93).

remember

Fig. 6. Join 4 rows.

MY ONE AND ONLY, 59" x 73", made by the author

My One and Only

Several years ago I made a memory quilt for my sister. This quilt had a panel with a poem on it that I framed out with a large border. I embroidered all the different memories I had of us growing up onto fabric and hand stitched them onto the quilt border. Some of these memories anyone who grew up with us would know, but some were special just between us. Her daughter, who was engaged, saw it and loved it. She asked me to make something like it for her and her fiancé. I had them write down all their special memories that they wanted to be included in the quilt. She included songs, concerts, special places, and so on. I embroidered them on squares that I made into a quilt and they now have an everlasting memory of their early years as a couple.

My One and Only was designed with that experience in mind, this time using my husband's and my memories of our early years together up until our marriage. It was so much fun looking back at that time and picking what we wanted to have memorialized in our quilt. Some of them will mean something to people who know us, but some have a special meaning that only Doug and I will know, and that is as it should be.

This design is perfect for these kinds of memory quilts and also for use as a signature quilt. The large blocks make it easy for anyone to sign, including children, and there is plenty of room for a special thought or wish for the recipient.

Fabric for an 18-Block 59" x 73" Quilt

Fabric Needed	Yardage
Dark purple	1½ yards
Yellow	1 yard
Light purple	1⅓ yards
White	1⅞ yards
Inner border	⅔ yard
Outer border	1¾ yards
Backing	5 yards
Binding	⅞ yard

Cutting Instructions

	Cutting Instructions
Dark purple	Cut 27 strips 1¾" wide. Cut 5 of the strips into 110 squares 1¾" x 1¾".
Yellow	Cut 14 strips 1¾" wide.
Light purple	Cut 8 strips 1¾" wide. Cut 5 strips 3⅜" wide into 55 squares 3⅜" x 3⅜". Cut the squares once in half on the diagonal to make 110 triangles.
White	Cut 5 strips 9½" wide into 18 squares 9½" x 9½". Cut 2 strips 5½" wide into 14 squares 5½" x 5½".
Inner border	Cut 6 strips 2½" wide.
Outer border	Cut 8 strips 6½" wide.
Binding	Cut 7 strips 2½" wide.

Step 1 – Make the center squares

a) Make a list of 18 memories or signatures you would like to put on your quilt.

Fig. 1. Use a template or ruler to center and level the design.

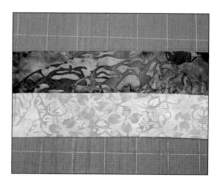

Fig. 2. Make 14 strip-sets.

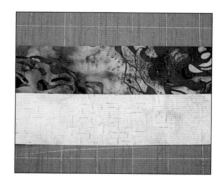

Fig. 3. Make 8 strip-sets.

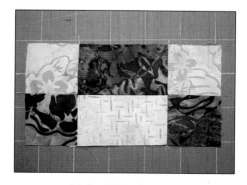

Fig. 4. Make 96 units.

Trish's Tip: I recommend that you do not put the quilt together until these center squares are totally completed, as the quilt top will be too bulky to pass around to be signed easily or to do the embroideries. Also, if someone makes a mistake in the writing it's easier to fix before the quilt is assembled. Patience here avoids aggravation and disappointment later.

b) Design the embroideries on your machine or in your favorite design program. You can use any font or size that you like as long as the embroidery does not go outside the 5" finished square size. I used the Calligraph 15–50mm font with the letters 13–21 mm tall. This gives an elegant, yet readable, embroidery.

IMPORTANT- The finished block will be set on point so you must design your embroideries to fit in the square when it is oriented this way.

Trish's Tip: If you do not have an embroidery machine, see if a friend will do the embroideries for you, with you supplying all the materials and thread. You could even offer to hand sew a binding for her while she is doing the embroideries for you!

c) If you are doing a signature quilt, cut the center square 9½" x 9½", then use a wash/iron away pen to outline the 5" x 5" square for the signatures to stay within. This provides a visual guide to signers for what will be visible in the quilt.

d) Trim the signed or embroidered squares to measure 5½" x 5½", making sure the design is centered. Remove any guidelines following the manufacturer's instructions (Fig. 1).

Step 2 – Cut the fabrics

Using the chart on page 75, cut the fabrics for the pieced blocks, sashing, borders, and binding.

Step 3 - Make the pieced blocks

a) Make 14 strip-sets with the 1¾" wide dark purple and yellow strips. Press the seams towards the dark fabric (Fig. 2).

b) Cut the strip-sets into 302 segments 1¾" wide.

c) Make 8 strip-sets with the 1¾" wide dark purple and light purple strips. Press the seams towards the dark fabric (Fig. 3).

d) Cut the strip-sets into 96 segments 3" wide.

e) Make 96 units of 1 dark purple/light purple segment and 2 dark purple/yellow segments each (Fig. 4).

f) Sew 2 units to each of your 18 blocks along the top left and bottom right sides. Press the seams toward the block (Fig. 5).

g) Add a 1¾" dark purple square to the remaining 110 dark purple/yellow segments to create L-shaped units. Press the seam toward the dark purple (Fig. 6).

h) Sew one of these L-shaped units to the left and right sides of 36 dark purple/yellow/light purple units to make corner edge units (Fig. 7). Press. (You'll have 38 L-shaped units left.)

i) Sew 2 corner edge units to the remaining 2 sides of the center squares (Fig. 8). Press.

Fig. 5. Add 2 units to each block.

Fig. 6. Make 110 L-shaped units.

Fig. 7. Make 36 corner edge units.

Fig. 8. The block set on point

Fig. 9. Cut the corners straight across.

Fig. 10. Position the light purple points as shown.

9/12/73

Fig. 11. The finished block. Make 18.

j) Place a ruler across the corners of the blocks as shown and trim the corners so they are straight across (Fig. 9).

k) Place light purple triangles at each corner making sure the points of the purple triangles are aligned with the points of the center square (Fig. 10).

l) Sew the triangles. Press the seam toward the triangles (Fig. 11).

m) Arrange your finished blocks on a design board according to the quilt layout diagram.

Quilt layout

Easy Memorabilia QUILTS: *ties, t-shirts, photos & more* – Trish Bowman

Step 4 – Make the side blocks

a) Add an L-shaped unit to the right edge of 10 dark purple/yellow/light purple units (Fig. 12). (You'll have 14 L-shaped units left.)

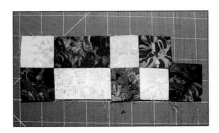

Fig. 12. An L-shaped piece is added to the right edge.

b) Sew one of these pieced units to one side of 10 white 5½" x 5½" squares. Press toward the white squares (Fig. 13).

c) Add an L-shaped unit to both edges of the remaining 14 dark purple/yellow/light purple units. Set aside 4 units for the corner blocks.

Fig. 13. Partially pieced side block

d) Pin 10 of these pieced units to the adjacent side of the partially pieced side blocks, matching the seams, and sew. Press away from the plain square (Fig. 14).

Fig. 14. Second unit added to the side block

f) Place a ruler across each of the three corners as shown and cut the corners so they are straight across (Figs. 15a and b).

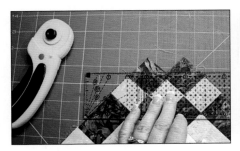

Figs. 15a and b. Trim the corners.

g) Place light purple triangles on the corners. Sew and press to complete the side blocks (Fig. 16).

h) Place your half blocks on the design board along the sides and top and bottom of your layout (Fig. 17, page 80).

Fig. 16. The completed side block. Make 10.

Fig. 17. Placing the side blocks

Fig. 18. The completed corner blocks.

Step 5 – Make the corner blocks

a) Take the 4 units you set aside earlier for the corner blocks. Trim the corners as before and add a triangle to both edges.

b) Sew this pieced unit to one side of the remaining 5½" x 5½" white squares (Fig. 18).

c) Place your half blocks on the design board at the four corners of your layout (Fig. 19).

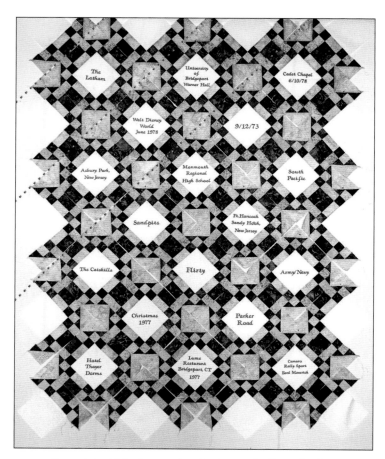

Fig. 19. Completed blocks on the design wall. Sew the blocks in diagonal rows (dashed lines).

Step 6 – Join the blocks

a) Sew the blocks into diagonal rows (Fig. 19, page 80).

b) Sew the rows together.

Step 7 - Trim the edges of the quilt

a) To evenly trim the edges of the quilt, line up a ruler on the diagonal of the center white squares of all the blocks on each side of the quilt (Fig. 20).

b) Cut along your ruler leaving a nice straight edge for your quilt (Fig. 21).

Fig. 20. Line up the ruler on the diagonal of the white squares.

Step 8 – Add the inner and outer borders
(page 30)

Your quilt top is complete!

Step 9 - Finishing

a) See Don't Forget the Back (pages 88–90).

b) Quilt as desired.

c) Add binding and a sleeve (pages 91–93).

Fig. 21. Finished inner quilt top

HE'S THE BOSS, 58" x 70", made by the author

Easy Memorabilia QUILTS: *ties, t-shirts, photos & more* – Trish Bowman

HE'S THE BOSS

Well, he thinks he is the boss, and most of the time we don't let them know any different, even though we all know who the boss really is. Many of us have husbands, dads, and grandfathers who wear ties everyday of their lives for work, church, or just because they like how it makes them feel, like us in a new pair of sexy shoes. This quilt was designed for that kind of guy—the one you never think about without thinking of him in his ties. It is the perfect gift for the man in your life who is retiring and swears he will never wear another tie.

While this design as presented is totally made from ties, you could easily mix it up and include fabric from his suits and shirts in it as well, making it into a clothes quilt and not just a tie quilt.

Fabric Requirements

Fabric Needed	Yardage
Ties for braids	30 plus
Sashing	⅞ yard
Flange	½ yard
Inner border	½ yard
Outer border	1¾ yards
Backing	4¾ yards
Binding	⅔ yard

Cutting Instructions

	Cutting Instructions
Ties	Cut strips 2½" x length of the ties into 168 rectangles 2½" x 8".
Sashing	Cut 5 strips 4" wide.
Flange	Cut 8 strips 1" wide.
Inner border	Cut 6 strips 2" wide.
Outer border	Cut 8 strips 6½" wide.
Binding	Cut 7 strips 2½" wide.

Fig. 1. Remove the stabilizer and press open.

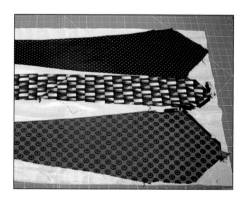

Fig. 2. Apply the tricot to the back of the ties.

Step 1 – Prepare the ties for the quilt

Trish's Tip: The number of ties needed will change based on the size of the ties. If the ties are wide and long for a tall man, you will of course need fewer than those from a shorter man or one who wore narrow ties.

a) Using a seam ripper, open the backs of the ties and remove the stabilizer. Press the tie open (Fig. 1).

b) Apply tricot to back of the ties according to manufacturer's directions. Do this by placing multiple ties on a single sheet of tricot (Fig. 2).

Trish's Tip: If you alternate the wide and narrow ends of the ties, you should be able to get three ties across the width of a 20" piece of tricot. This will save time and decrease the amount of waste.

Step 2 - Cut ties into fabric strips

Cut the ties according to the cutting instructions. You will need 21 sets of tie strips for a total of 42 strips per braid.

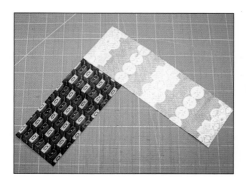

Fig. 3. Connect 2 tie strips.

Step 3 – Piece the ties into braided rows

> **Trish's Tip:** When making this quilt be sure to use as little steam as possible on the ties. It is important to PRESS, not iron, so the tie fabric strips don't stretch out of shape. If you get a little stretching that ultimately causes some bubbles in the quilt top, you can usually take care of this while quilting the quilt.

Fig. 4. Continue adding the strips.

a) Place 2 strips of tie fabric at a 90-degree angle. Stitch them together and press (Fig. 3).

b) Continue adding strips, alternating left and right sides, pressing toward the newly added strip (Fig. 4).

c) Use 42 strips on each braid. Make 4 braids (Fig. 5).

Step 4 – Trim the braids

a) Lay your ruler on top of the braid, lining it up so the 4" line goes through the center points of the braid in a straight line (Fig. 6, page 86).

b) Use a rotary cutter to trim the right side of the braid (Fig. 7, page 86).

Fig. 5. Pieced braid

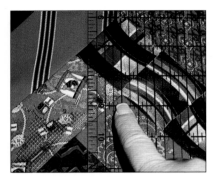

Fig. 6. Align the 4" line with the points of the braid.

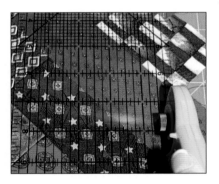

Fig. 7. Trim the side of the braid.

Fig. 8. Two braids with trimmed edges. Make 4.

Fig. 9. Sashing strip with a flange attached to both sides

c) Repeat on the other side. Trim the ends. The braids should measure 8" x 55" (Fig. 8).

Step 5 – Make sashing for between braids

a) Piece the 4" sashing strips with 45-degree seams as needed (page 29).

b) Cut 3 sashing strips the length of the braids.

Step 6 – Make flanges for sides of sashing

a) Piece the flange strips with 45-degree seams. Fold the strips in half lengthwise and press.

b) Cut the flange strips the same length as the sashings. Pin a flange to the side of a sashing strip, matching the raw edges.

c) Sew the flange to the sashing with a scant ¼" seam so the stitching will not show in the finished quilt. Repeat this on the other side of the sashing (Fig. 9).

Trish's Tip: If you are going to have your quilt machine quilted you will need to baste down the inner side of the flange so it will not get pulled up during the quilting process. Once it is quilted you will pull out the basting threads.

d) Add flanges to the sides of the 2 remaining sashing strips.

Step 7 — Sew the braids and sashing together

Pin the sashings and the braids together and stitch. Referring to the photo (page 82), you can see that I alternated the direction the ties pointed to get a different pattern. You can arrange your braids that way or oriented all in the same direction.

> **Trish's Tip:** Make sure you pin the ends and the middle first, and then pin all the seams very well. Tie fabric, even stabilized, still has a lot of give due to the way it is cut and can easily stretch. The more pins you use in this step to ease things together the better off you will be.

Step 8 — Add the inner and outer borders (page 30)

Your quilt top is complete!

Step 9 - Finishing

a) See Don't Forget the Back (pages 88–90).

b) Quilt as desired.

c) Add binding and a sleeve (pages 91–93).

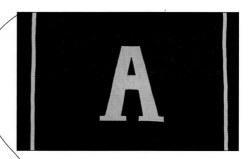

Fig. 1. Detail of the back of a West Point memory quilt

Fig. 2. Detail of the back of an Army/Navy game memory quilt

Fig. 3. Back of Kyoto Ring quilt

I have often thought that the most neglected part of a quilt is the back. So many quilters concentrate all their efforts on the front of their quilts and are so happy to finally have the quilt done that they don't put any real effort into the back. Many times they don't even put on a label. I have to admit I can be one of those people. In a lot of my quilts I just found some nice matching fabric and used it for the back. In the past I have also been one of those naughty quilters who didn't always label my quilts. I really regret that and now am very conscientious about putting a label on all my quilts.

I love it when I have an idea for how I can carry over the theme or design on the front of the quilt to the back. Sometimes it is just in a fun label and other times it is something that takes over the entire back. As you are making your quilts, think about the back and see what ideas flow into your head. As you will see, the possibilities are endless.

Let's take the backs themselves. I carried over the theme of a memory quilt I did for my husband out of his West Point uniforms and fabric with a large Army A appliquéd on the back (Fig. 1).

On the front of this memory quilt are many of the Army/Navy football game T-shirts we collected during the first decade of our life together. I felt it was only appropriate that I appliqué our favorite saying on the back (Fig. 2). Both of these quilts go to every game with us. We always get smiles from people when they see them and they definitely keep us warm!

I made a Kyoto Ring quilt (pattern by Carolyn Leuboldt, Syzille, NY) and wanted to do something special on the back. I went online and looked up the Chinese symbols for love, hope, and faith and put them on the back. It wasn't difficult and it added a nice touch to the back (Fig. 3).

I made an Oklahoma Sooners baby quilt for a family member and my son, Christopher, gave me the idea of putting the covered wagon on the back (Fig. 4). It was the perfect touch. My family is great at giving me ideas for my quilts.

Since Doug loves trains I have lots of different train fabrics. I found this panel in my stash and decided to make it the focus of the back (Fig. 5).

When I made the quilt REACH FOR THE STARS, the space shuttle program was coming to an end. I thought of this design for the back. It looks complicated, but it is a very simple appliqué adapted from photos (Fig. 6).

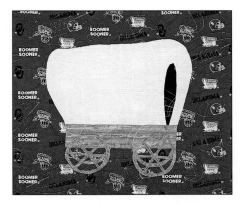

Fig. 4. Detail of the back of a quilt made for Oklahoma Sooners fans

Fig. 5. Detail of the back of I PLAY WITH TRAINS, full quilt on page 32

Fig. 6. Detail of the back of REACH FOR THE STARS, full quilt on page 42

Fig. 7. Label on REACH FOR THE STARS (page 42)

Labels

Labels can be much more than just functional. These examples are not hard to do. They just take a little extra time.

The themes of many of my quilts get carried over to the labels.

Fig. 8. KYOTO RING quilt label

Fig. 9. Label on a Pinwheel quilt

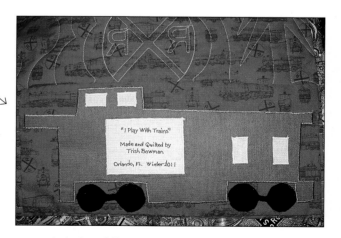

Fig. 10. Label on I PLAY WITH TRAINS (page 32)

Fig. 11. Label on a puppy-themed quilt

The last thing to do is to bind your quilt and put a sleeve on it if you are going to hang it at home or in a show. If you are just hanging it at home you can do whatever works for you, but if you plan on putting your quilt in a show, most require a certain kind of sleeve to fit over their poles.

Binding your quilt

a) Cut your strips 2½" wide and piece them as you would borders, page 30. Press the strips in half lengthwise, wrong sides together, opening and pressing the seams as you go.

b) Apply the binding by lining up the raw edge of the binding with the trimmed edge of your quilt. Start sewing about halfway across the bottom of the quilt. Leave about 5" of binding free to connect when you finish going around the quilt.

c) When you get to the corners, stop stitching ¼" from the end and backstitch a few stitches (Fig. 1).

d) Remove the quilt from the machine and fold the unsewn end of the binding straight up off the corner (Fig. 2).

e) Fold the binding back down, making sure that the top of the fold is even with the edge

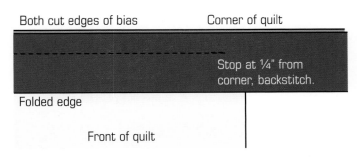

Fig. 1. Stop stitching ¼" from end and backstitch

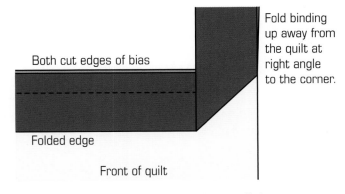

Fig. 2. Fold the unsewn end straight up off the corner.

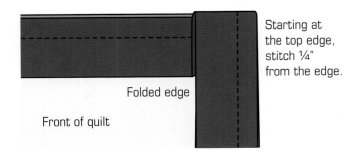

Fig. 3. Fold back down even with the quilt edge and stitch.

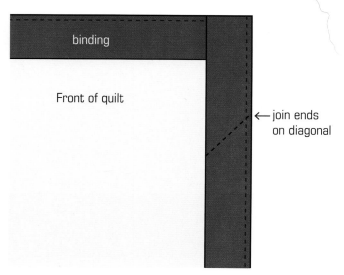

binding

Front of quilt

← join ends
on diagonal

Fig. 4

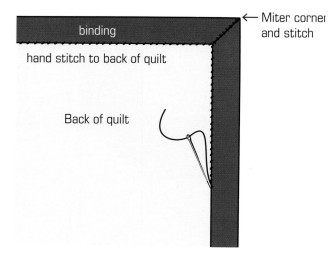

← Miter corner
and stitch

binding

hand stitch to back of quilt

Back of quilt

Fig. 5

of the quilt and the raw edges of the binding are lined up with the next side of the quilt. The 45-degree angle should be intact under the fold (Fig. 3, page 91).

f) Start sewing at the top edge and continue in this manner until you have gone all the way around the quilt (Fig. 3, page 91).

g) When you get to the bottom again stop sewing on the binding about 5" from where you started and backstitch a few stitches.

h) Bring the binding ends together and finger press to mark where your seam should be to sew together the two ends of the binding.

i) Open both ends of the binding and, using the press markings, stitch the two ends together along the fold mark. Trim the seam to ¼" and finger press open.

j) Sew the rest of the binding down (Fig. 4).

k) Fold the binding to the back and hand stitch in place, making sure you miter your corners nicely (Fig. 5).

Making a hanging sleeve

a) Measure the top of your quilt edge-to-edge.

b) Cut a strip 9" x the width of your quilt.

c) Fold in the short ends ¼" and again another ¼" to enclose the raw edge. Sew along the folded edge.

d) Fold the strip in half lengthwise, wrong sides together, and press.

e) Open the strip and fold the long edges of the fabric into the center fold, wrong sides together. Press the edges well.

f) Turn the fabric so the right sides are together and sew down the long open edge, resulting in a tube.

g) Turn the tube right-side out.

h) Pin the sleeve to the back of the quilt about ¾" from the top, using the previously pressed in folds as your edges for pinning it down. You will notice when doing this that a bubble or D will appear in the sleeve. This is just what you need to hang your quilt on any rod.

i) Hand stitch the sleeve to the quilt. Go around all four edges including the part of the sleeve at the opening that sits on the quilt back. Make sure your stitches go through the backing and the batting but not through to the front of the quilt.

Detail of the back of REACH FOR THE STARS. Full quilt on page 42.

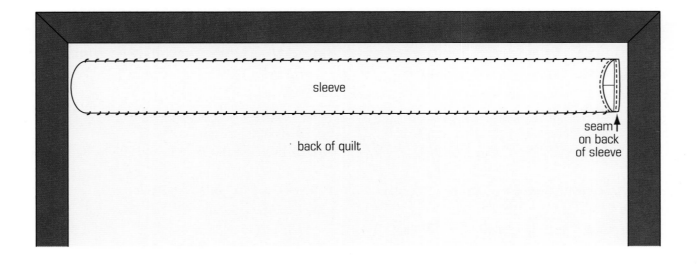

sleeve

back of quilt

seam on back of sleeve

resources

Trish Bowman	New Leaf Stitches
www.trishbowman.com	www.newleafstitches.com
All Squared Up Tee's Templates	Clearly Perfect Angles (Patent Pending)
Row Marking Safety Pins	

fabrics used

Fabrics Used in I PLAY WITH TRAINS

RJR Fabrics, by Dan Morris 2011, Just Train Crazy,
   #0838-01. Wide Border
All Aboard designed for Exclusively Quilters –
   Red used for sashing
Red Hen Fabrics #8766 licensed by Lionel LLC – Backing

Fabrics Used in REACH FOR THE STARS

Front:
   Hoffman Fabrics, Bali Watercolor #1895,
      Color #293 Fox
   Hoffman Fabrics, Bali Watercolor #1895,
      Color # 451 Cornflower
   Benartex, Space: The New Frontier, Style # 04416
   Benartex, Space: The New Frontier, Panel Style
      #04415
   Robert Kaufman, Mixmasters,
      Luminescence screen print, D#10835
Back:
   Hoffman California International Fabrics,
      "Inter Cosmic", Style # H8746

Fabrics Used in SAILING THE OCEAN BLUE

Tempting Tonals by Fabric Freedom in London, England,
   Color Blue F745
Hoffman Fabrics, Style # 1895, Cornflower, light blue
Hoffman Fabrics, Style # 1895, Waikilki, dark blue

Fabrics Used in DIVIDED BY SERVICE, UNITED BY LOVE

Robert Kaufman – "Patriots" Screen Print D#5238,
   Air Force Fabric

Robert Kaufman – "Patriots" Screen Print D#5237,
   Army Fabric
Robert Kaufman – "Patriots" Screen Print D#5240,
   Navy Fabric
Maywood Studios - Solitaire Whites V,
   Stars MAS209-OW
Blue Hill Fabrics – The Empire Collection,
   Designed by Rose Studios. SKU 7223-2
Backing – Susan Winget – CP3687, Patriotic

Fabric Used in THOSE WERE THE DAYS

Garden Song by Nancy Halvorsen, Benartex,
   Style # 04283-30, Gold
Rambling Favorites 2005, by P & B Textiles,
   White-on-White
Kona Elegence by Robert Kaufman, CPC 10991-167,
   Chocolate
Symphony Dark Chocolate, Joann's 400105482129
   (used in single photo frame)
Printed Treasures – Inkjet Printable Fabric

Fabrics Used in MY ONE AND ONLY QUILT

Bavarian Batiks by Wilmington Prints, Light Purple
Tartans Violet
Artisan Batiks by Robert Kaufman, Pineapple
Bali Handpaints by Hoffman, Peony
Rambling Feathers, by P & B Textiles, White-on-White

Fabrics Used in HE'S THE BOSS

Complements, Bella Lu Studio Licensed to SSI,
   by South Sea Imports
Linen Texture by P & B Textiles, Red

meet Trish Bowman

Trish Bowman has been sewing and doing all kinds of crafts for over 40 years. The craft bug came from her mom. In high school she became a serious seamstress, starting out by making her own clothes, progressing to reupholstering furniture, and eventually making clothes for her husband. Never one to sit and enjoy the status quo, she was always experimenting with new techniques and challenges, discovering quilting in the mid-1980s. Her love affair with this new dimension of her hobby blossomed as she realized quilting offered a better outlet for her creativity than making clothes.

In the more than quarter century since, Trish has made hundreds of quilts. Her favorite quilts have always been the ones that held people's memories. Her first T-shirt quilt, created in 1988, was for her husband and celebrated his days in college by using old T-shirts that otherwise would have gone to the rag bin. Subsequently, she has made many memory quilts for family, friends, and, more recently, clients.

In addition to working on her own or clients' creations, Trish can frequently be found helping friends and guild members who are inspired to make their own memory quilts and need some extra help and advice. As an experienced quilter, Trish recognizes that she has learned from and been inspired by the many quilters she has interacted with over the years. The desire to help others do what she loves, just as others helped her, was the inspiration for writing a book to provide flexible and useful designs and techniques for making T-shirt and memory quilts.

Today, Trish has a studio full of books and fabrics and a Gammill Statler Stitcher to finish all the quilts she makes. A member of the Florida Cabin Fever Quilt Guild, she has served as president and Cabin Fever Quilt Show chairperson. As owner of Jersey Girl Quilts, a custom quilt business, she designs and makes memory quilts for clients who don't want to or can't make their own. Based on her experiences with this business, a ruler/template system was developed that eases the cutting of shirts and improves cutting accuracy over the use of a basic square ruler.

Trish lives in central Florida with her husband of 34 years, Doug, and their puppy, Penny. She has two grown children, Christopher and Jennifer, a son-in-law, Michael, and is anxiously awaiting her first grandchild in 2013. She is a registered nurse and successfully ran her own legal nurse consulting business prior to moving to Florida 10 years ago.

Learn more about Trish at her website: **www.trishbowman.com**

more AQS books

This is only a small selection of the books available from the American Quilter's Society. AQS books are known worldwide for timely topics, clear writing, beautiful color photos, and accurate illustrations and patterns. The following books are available from your local bookseller, quilt shop, or public library.

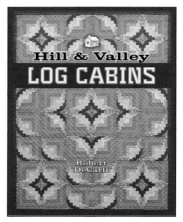

#1246

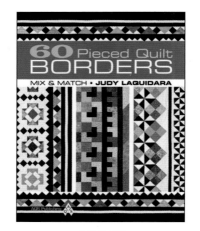

#8662

#8532

#8523

#8347

#8664

#8665

#1245

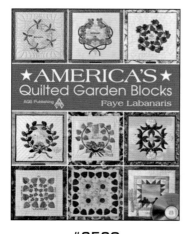

#8530